MOTHER OF ALL THE BEHANS

Brian Behan, the third son of Kathleen and Stephen Behan, was born in 1927 and educated at a boarding school till he was fourteen. In 1969 he went to Sussex University as a mature student. He has been a public speaker at many universities, including Trinity College, Dublin, Oxford and Cambridge. He was also a radical trade unionist for many years, and as such visited the Soviet Union, where he met Stalin, and China, where he met Mao.

Brian Behan has written widely for magazines such as *Tribune* and the *Spectator*, and is the author of two radio plays. His own autobiography, *WITH BREAST EXPANDED*, was published in 1964.

Brian Behan now lives in London, and lectures at the London College of Printing.

D1028822

Brian Behan

MOTHER OF ALL THE BEHANS

The autobiography of Kathleen Behan
as told to Brian Behan

An Arena Book

Published by Arrow Books Limited
17-21 Conway Street, London W1P 6JD

An imprint of the Hutchinson Publishing Group

London Melbourne Sydney Auckland
Johannesburg and agencies throughout
the world

First published by Hutchinson 1984
Arena edition 1985

Printed and bound in Great Britain
by the Guernsey Press Co. Ltd,
Guernsey, C.I.

ISBN 0 09 940470 4

Contents

Chronological Table

1889 Kathleen B. Kearney, the third child of John Kearney and Katie McGuinness, born at 49 Capel Street, Dublin, on 18 September

1898 Enters orphanage, a dull cold place on a dull cold day

1904 Leaves orphanage

1916 Marries Jack Furlong, a printer (compositor)

1917 First son, Rory, born

1918 Death of first husband, Jack Furlong
Birth of Sean Furlong
As young widow, obtains work with Dublin Corporation

1919 Meets Stephen Behan

1920 Works for Whitecross (Republican Aid Association)

1922 Marries Stephen Behan
Moves to Russell Street

1923 Brendan Behan born

1925 Seamus Behan born

1927 Brian Behan born

1929 Dominic Behan born

1931 Brendan joins Fianna Eirran (Republican Scout Organization founded by Madame Markievicz)

1932 Carmel Behan, only daughter, born
Election of De Valera to power

1933 Death of Christina Behan (the Grannie)

1937 Brendan volunteers to fight in Spain on the Republican side

The Behans leave Russell Street and emigrate to Crumlin

Brendan's first article published in *An Phoblact* (*The Republic*)

1939   Brendan arrested in Liverpool

1944   Brendan transferred to Curragh internment camp

1946   Brendan released from prison in general amnesty

Rory leaves Free State Army. Emergency is declared over

Brendan is a housepainter, seaman and sometime smuggler

1947   Brendan goes to the Blasket Island, Kerry, and lays basis for *Brendan Behan's Island*

Brendan arrested in Manchester for attempting to free an IRA man from prison

Brendan released from the same prison that had held his Grannie Furlong and Aunt Emily, who had been jailed for running a safe house for the IRA bomb campaign

1948   Brendan sentenced to one month's hard labour for assaulting a policeman

Brendan moves to Paris

1950   Brian Behan goes to England

1951   Sean Furlong follows

1951–2   Dominic and Carmel go to England

1952   Brendan arrested at Newhaven, Sussex, for evading a deportation order

Released from six-month sentence at Lewes prison, Sussex

1953   Seamus goes to England

1954   Alan Simpson directs *The Quare Fellow* at the Pike Theatre, Dublin

1955   Brendan marries Beatrice ffrench-Salkeld, daughter of the Irish artist Cecil Salkeld, at the Sacred Heart Church, Donybrook

1956   *The Quare Fellow*, directed by Joan Littlewood, opens at the Theatre Royal, Stratford, East London

Borstal Boy published serially in the Irish edition of the *Sunday Despatch*

The Quare Fellow published
1957 *The Hostage*, directed by Joan Littlewood, opens at the
Theatre Royal, Stratford, East London
Borstal Boy published
The Quare Fellow, directed by Jose Quintero, opens off
Broadway, New York
The Hostage published
1959 *The Hostage* moves to Wyndham's Theatre in the West
End of London
Brendan's first serious breakdown
1960 *Brendan Behan's Island* taped in Dublin
1961 Brendan travels 11,000 miles across the United States
and Canada
Two periods in hospital
Brendan returns to Dublin
1962 *Brendan Behan's Island* published
Brendan goes to France to recuperate
Returns to Dublin after failure of cure
1963 Brendan's final trip to America
Brendan tapes *Confessions of an Irish Rebel* in New York
Hold your Hour and Have Another published
Brendan Behan's New York taped in Dublin
Blanaid Behan born
Brendan enters hospital. Later released
1964 Brendan dies in Meath Hospital, Dublin
1967 Stephen Behan, Kathleen's second husband, dies
1970 Kathleen Behan appears on Irish Television (Gay Byrne
Show)
Leaves her home in Crumlin, having lived there for
thirty-three years, and goes into Sacred Heart
Residence at Sibyl Hill
1979 Her birthday is celebrated by leading Dubliners at the
Embankment Tallagh. She is now ninety
1981 Release of her first long-playing record, 'When all the
world was young'
1984 Publication of Kathleen's autobiography *Mother of All
the Behans*

Illustrations

Between pages 80 and 81

BEHAN FAMILY TREE

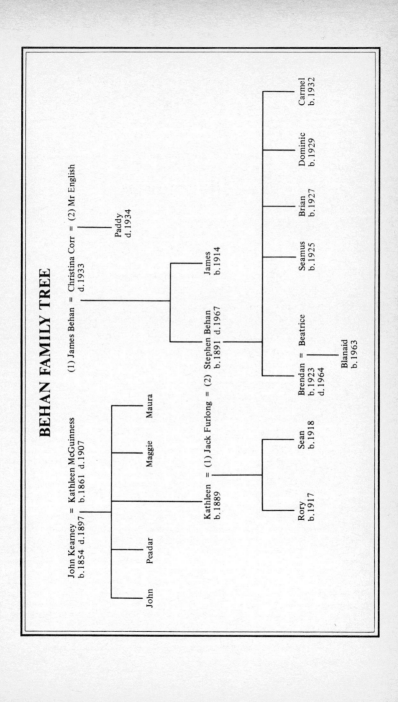

(1) James Behan = Christina Corr = (2) Mr English
                             d.1933

Paddy
d.1934

James
b.1914

John Kearney = Kathleen McGuinness
b.1854 d.1897   b.1861 d.1907

John   Peadar   Maggie   Maura

Kathleen = (1) Jack Furlong = (2) Stephen Behan
b.1889   b.1891 d.1967

Rory   Sean
b.1917   b.1918

Brendan = Beatrice   Seamus   Brian   Dominic   Carmel
b.1923   b.1925   b.1927   b.1929   b.1932
d.1964

Blanaid
b.1963

Foreword

'All my mother's geese were swans'

My mother is as Dublin as the hills. For a number of years I tried to persuade her to write her autobiography, but she refused, mainly because she couldn't be bothered and, I suspect, was far too busy living. She had been approached many times by many people who wanted to write a biography of her, but she had always turned them down on the grounds that this would be far too personal: interviews, radio spots and television appearances she performed with great gusto, but at the same time she felt that a biography, however favourable, might reveal parts of her life about which she felt very keenly. I approached her in the spring of 1979, asking her to think about it again. Finally, later, I decided to have a go at it myself, and to my surprise she agreed quite willingly, because she felt that she might not be allowed much more time and just as kindly felt that she might be helping me. For that feeling I am truly grateful.

My mother often said that there is no love like that of a mother. It supports, it engulfs, it encourages, it swamps. In my own case I owe to my mother the very great measure of self-confidence with which I am blessed. She told me at a very early age, 'There is no one on earth any better than you. As good, maybe, but certainly no better.' That thought, that in this whole wide world there was no one better than me, I felt roll under me like a supporting raft that enabled me to navigate stormy waters from here to Shanghai. All my mother's geese were swans.

The fact that Kathleen Behan is 'the mother of all the Behans' is not the only reason for writing her life story. Her life embraces almost a century of Irish history. My mother was a young girl in the city of George Bernard Shaw, Oscar Wilde and Oliver St John Gogarty. James Joyce, the wordsmith of *Dubliners*, *Ulysses* and *Finnegans Wake*, and Sean O'Casey, the author of *Juno and the Paycock* and *The Plough and the Stars*, lived near the tenement home of my childhood.

My mother, born in the paralysed city of Joyce, lived to see it burn in the flames of the Rebellion. Her Dublin was also the city of Larkin, the great trade union organizer, and Connolly, the Marxist, who led the Citizen Army into a seemingly impossible Nationalist revolution. In all this my mother and her family played an important part. Her brother, Peadar Kearney, composed the National Anthem. As she says herself, 'All the men of my family were out in Easter Week.' This Republican–Labour tradition she encouraged by rocking her children in the cradle to the air of 'The Red Flag' and 'Let Erin Remember'. A rebel woman, she fought for the rights of women when such things were not fashionable. The reader may feel that here is material for not one book, but ten. I have tried to compress it all within this single offering.

The book is a collaboration between my mother and myself, with help from others. It contains my mother's thoughts in response to my questions, tape recorded at her home in the Residence of the Sacred Heart in Dublin. It is, on occasion, a self-contradictory record, for these are the thoughts and feelings of a very old woman. But the strength and gaiety with which they are expressed seemed to me to justify inconsistencies. And anyway, inconsistency is the key to a poor person's survival.

The home she now lives in is a fine one, for the elderly, standing on the brow of Raheny Hill. From my mother's room you can see the bay of Dublin she loves so well, and beyond it rise the Dublin Mountains. She went into the home, as she put it, '. . . to save myself from being a burden to any of you'. She finds her life there a lonely one – comfortable, wanting for nothing in creature comforts, but yet lonely. A feature of our lives is that, as rapidly as possible, we consign our old to anywhere so long as they don't trouble us. And yet we will all be old some day. The home is run by nuns, and they were kind enough to allow me to make the recordings in their rooms. To them I offer my thanks.

Many others have helped with reminiscences and support when I was compiling the book, although I take full responsibility for any remaining inaccuracies. If I have omitted to mention any of them, I plead forgiveness. My thanks go to:

Rory, my eldest brother, who fought for the book through thick and thin.

My brother Seamus, for helpful support.

Beatrice and Blanaid Behan, wife and daughter respectively of Brendan, for all their very great assistance with research and written material. Beatrice has contributed an appreciation of Kathleen which is printed at the end of the book.

Carmel, our only sister, for her help and encouragement.

Jimmy Burke, Dublin historical author and beloved cousin.

Rae Jeffs and David Astor, for their reminiscences.

Mick Coogan, an old Dubliner and lifelong family friend, without whose stories the book would have been the poorer.

Liam Flynn, Art Editor of *The Irish Press*, for his ungrudging assistance.

E.H. Mikhail and Macmillan/Gill and Macmillan for Da's reminiscences of Brendan, quoted in *Brendan Behan: Interviews and Recollections*, and for chronological information about Brendan's career.

Margaret Bond and Abigail Frost.

And last but not least, Tony Whittome, who teased this book out of a mountain of impressions.

Introduction

*'If you can survive your own family
you can survive anything'*

I've been almost fifteen years in this home now. I came in when I was eighty. I used only to eat and sleep here, and go out during the day. I've always liked it here. The people are my friends – you're never short of someone to talk to. Living on your own you'd go mad, wouldn't you? I am not a good mixer, though. Mrs Brown (the woman in the next room) and I have always been good friends, but I don't mix much with the others.

I would never have come in here at all, but for my accident. Once I had been knocked down I couldn't do for myself. My eye was nearly knocked out and one of my legs was broken. The driver of the motorcycle was in a hurry to get back to work for half one. I was stepping off the path and he ploughed into me. I was in hospital for a year – I had to be taught how to walk all over again.

My husband Stephen died the day after I was knocked down. It all happened together. My son Rory came up to see me and he was crying. I knew then that something had happen to Da – that's what we all called Stephen. I was ill for two years after, and I couldn't manage on my own with Da gone, so I finally gave up the house and here I am.

I'm well used to this place now; they do everything for us. They feed you, bath you, scrub you and everything. I used not to like anyone to see me undressed, and for five years I stood and washed myself as best I could. I used to pretend to the

17

nuns that I had had a bath, but it wouldn't be a proper bath, sure it wouldn't.

The only fault I find with this place is that it's very early for a woman of ninety-five to get up. They start to dress us at seven and I have to go very slowly on account of my age. All I take for breakfast is a little bit of bread and a cup of tea. I don't go to Mass now – Mass comes up to me. It's piped up and you can stay in your room and listen. It's as good as going. It all comes up on the loudspeakers – four Masses in the morning. You could get sick of Masses. I haven't become any more religious as time has gone on. Still, I have no fears, not even of death. What I wouldn't like is a long illness.

> And when Sergeant Death in his cold arms embrace me,
> And lull me to sleep in sweet Eireann go Bradh,
> I will forget not O'Grady, the bard of Armagh.
> When cold Sergeant Death embraces me I will go gladly.

I like the priest here. He's a lovely man, and he hears my confession now and again. Not like some of the priests I remember. I didn't like their sermons – not at all – as we were always being damned. My brother Peadar was in church one time and the priest was shouting off the altar, saying that we were all damned. Peadar shouted back at him, 'Yes, we're damned all right. Like all the poor in this country, damned with hunger!'

I heard a priest preach off the altar in England, saying that the Queen needed our blessing. I walked out of the church. He came to me afterwards, saying it was a terrible thing to do. I told him I couldn't stand in the house of God and listen to that. I said, 'The Queen doesn't need anyone's blessing. She's blessed enough already with great riches, land and everything else.'

During the Spanish Civil War we got into trouble with the priests. They called to the house to get a collection up for the Fascists. Well, Da effed the priests out of it. They shouted back at us, 'You'll all burn in the flames of Hell for eternity!' It was a desperate cold winter's night and Da just laughed and shouted after them, 'Well, at least we'll be effing warm, which is more than we are here.'

Another time a priest came round to take up a collection for the black babies in Africa. He held out the box to me, the one with the little black child's head that nods every time you put a penny in. Well, I said nothing, and he looked at me.

'Mrs Behan,' says he, 'don't you want to help a heathen to see the face of God?'

'Don't they have enough gods of their own without us giving them another one?' says I, 'and besides that, aren't there enough white children running around the streets of Dublin in their bare feet? Shouldn't you collect for them first?'

I heard him say to someone else, 'I needn't go to her again, she's a Red.' That's what he said to everyone. 'We needn't knock on *her* door for a subscription again. She's a Red.'

I met him after and I said, 'Father, I am not red, I'm scarlet.'

I was born a Fenian and I hope to die a Fenian. I knew every word of 'God Save Ireland' when I was about six years old. My father was a Fenian too – the Lord have mercy on him.

But I don't support any political party. I only support causes. During the Spanish Civil War I supported the Republicans because they *were* Republicans. I don't support kings or queens, prime ministers or *Taoiseachs*. I have always supported the workers and will until I die. I think the Irishman is a great worker when he can get work. There's a woman here in the home with me. Well, she was talking to the doctor one day, and she said to him, 'Doctor, I love it in here. I had no life outside, you know.'

And the doctor said, 'Were you not married?'

She said, 'Oh yes, I was married.'

'Well then, had you a bad husband?' he asked.

'I had not a bad husband,' says she. 'He was a good man.'

'So then,' says the doctor, 'what made you unhappy?'

'Well, doctor,' says she, 'he was a turf picker, but he had no turf to pick.'

Isn't idleness a terrible thing?

The BBC interviewed me once and asked me if I thought my sons were troublemakers, causing strikes and all that. I said they didn't give the employers *half* enough trouble. Sure, the working man never got anything without struggling for it. The workers' song, 'The Red Flag', is a great song. Shall I sing it now?

> The workers' flag is deepest red;
> It shrouded oft our martyred dead
> And ere their limbs grew stiff and cold
> Their heart's blood dyed its every fold.
>
> Then raise the scarlet standard high
> Within its shade we'll live and die
> Though cowards flinch and traitors sneer
> We'll keep the red flag flying here.
>
> It hovered o'er our infant might
> When all around seemed dark as night
> It witnessed many a deed and vow
> We will not change its colour now.
>
> No worker can forget the day
> When Connolly stood 'mid war's array
> And raised aloft 'mid volleys three,
> That blood-stained flag of liberty.
> Rise, Irish workers, from your knees
> Fling forth your banners to the breeze
> See where its folds are tinged with red.
> That's blood our Irish workers shed.

That last verse is Peadar's. Your Uncle's workers' song.

I made a record there a while back, and the other day I got £130 off it. I put it in the bank in case I lost it: it can go towards my burial. Then I did all those television appearances – I did *The Late, Late Show* and *The Russell Harty Show*. Stephen was chosen once for *This Is Your Life*. Russell Harty was the last thing I did for television, and I wouldn't do any more – sure

I'm not able now. I haven't got the energy. I enjoyed Russell Harty very much, though. He wrote me a letter and all. I still have it. He was a lovely man. Very nice and polite he was. I got on great with him.

Up to now I have felt like a young girl. I suppose what's kept me young has been good humour, singing and dancing, and jumping around in general. If anyone wants to live to my age let them be happy and singing all the time. Let them avoid drink except a little. We're allowed a bottle of Guinness in here for a tonic, but I don't like it. One of the Guinness family said to our Brendan, 'We've been very good to the people of Dublin.' Our Brendan said, 'They've been even better to you.' I used to stop out with the Guinness family in their great big mansion. Brendan took me out there – who else? It was a lovely place with a long drive up to the house, set away back in the mountains so you would never know it's there. One of them said to Brendan, 'What's a socialist like you doing out here?' Brendan said, 'Learning to fulfil my ambition to be a rich Red.'

I cannot agree that things are much better in Ireland today than they were in the days before the Rising or just after it. The working classes never benefit from wars. Why, you look at today against forty years or so ago. Then Da could have had forty pints for a pound note. Today you wouldn't get one pint for a pound – you'd have to add a few bob more to it. There are more demands and pressures on today's people than there were in the old days. A tenement house room only cost you a few shillings, and you could usually buy a little meat, bread and butter, so you didn't starve. You had neighbours in the house, good people who would help out if you had any problems. You don't see that too much today. You didn't have to worry about paying for a car, a washing machine or a television, or about a son or daughter on drugs or in bad company. No, things are not better today. We could laugh, dance, sing and enjoy ourselves on very little in the old days. The people today lack all that, whether they have the money or not.

I made men of all my sons. Why was I so independent?

Well, I know other mothers were prepared to be slaves to their families, but I wasn't. I had to survive the break-up of our little family. Then I had to survive two wars, two husbands, the death of two of my sons. Da said I was the great survivor. I suppose if you can survive your own family you can survive anything.

Here's a song for you. It's called 'The Tri-colour Ribbon-oh'. I sang it to Gay Byrne. The time was up on the television, but they couldn't stop me, they let me carry on.

Oh, all around my hat I wear a tri-colour ribbon-oh,
All around my hat until death comes to me.
And if anyone should ask me why I'm wearing that green ribbon-oh,
It's all for my true love I ne'er more shall see.
He whispered, 'Goodbye, love, Old Ireland is calling,'
With his bandolier around him, his bright bayonet shining,
His short service rifle a beauty to see.
There was joy in his heart though he left me behind him,
And started away to make Old Ireland free.

Kathleen Behan,
Dublin, December 1983

1
Childhood

'We saw the two days, one wet, one fine'

Kathleen Kearney was born in Dublin, at the end of the 1880s, to parents who both came from relatively prosperous farming stock. With the death of her father in 1894, however, her comfortable early childhood came to an abrupt halt: her mother, unable to support the family at home, had to send Kathleen and her sisters to an orphanage

I was born at 49 Capel Street, Dublin, in September 1889. My grandparents had a farm: Rathmaiden, near Slane in County Meath, that's where our farm was. I used to go down for holidays regularly. Mother had a brother called John McGuinness – he inherited; he came into the farm, she didn't. Mother died very poor. She was born in 1861; the Famine was in 1845, and *her* mother lived all through it. She told my mother how she saw the canal boats weighed down with grain, while people starved along the banks. Was it not a terrible thing to do, to fatten cattle before people? I heard that the babies were drinking from their dead mothers' breasts. (I only heard that: what truth is in it I don't know.)

I learnt the ballads on the farm, when I was a young girl. The people would gather in at night for a chat around the fire. There would be about twenty there, but no Gaelic-speakers. They would talk about the farms, the animals and all that, and sing songs. Some were about the hard life they led. D'you remember 'Dan O'Hara'?

Oh, it's sad I am today, God gave and took away
And left without a home, poor Dan O'Hara.
In the frost and snow I stand, with my matches in my hand.
And it's sad I am today and broken-hearted.

Ah cushla gradh mo croidh, won't you buy a box from me
And you'll cheer the heart of Dan from Connemara?

25

I will sell them cheap and low.
Buy a box before you go
From the broken-hearted farmer Dan O'Hara.

In the year of 64, we had acres by the score
Of the finest land you ever set a plough through,
But the landlord came, you know, he laid our poor house low.
So it's sad, I am today, and broken-hearted.

Ah, cushla gradh mo croidh, won't you buy a box from me
And you'll cheer the heart of Dan from Connemara?
I will sell them cheap and low
Buy a box before you go
From the broken-hearted farmer Dan O'Hara.

When they all gathered tea would be made for them; I don't remember any drink, only tea. The people that used to come in at Rathmaiden were very happy. They would talk about things – times that were past – and then they would say a big long rosary with a long trimming. I'd think it would never end. You know what the rosary is – prayers to save our immortal souls. I said enough prayers then to last me all my life. I was very young to have to be kneeling there listening to all this – I must have been about seven.

They used to dance at the crossroads, but I remember once the priest would not allow the dancing. He thought they were carrying on, but they were only enjoying themselves. He thought the dancing was sinful, so he banned it. At the Sunday morning Mass he read it off the altar – he simply told them not to go dancing at the corners. There is a song about those Masses:

At the Sunday Mass where the neighbours met to tell their tidings,
A few are left of all the throng that used to crowd the door.
A few brave hearts, a few grey heads,
But not a face, with will to chase
The woe from us no more.

My mother had only the one brother, and he died young at thirty-six and left eight children. The boys all went to

America, and the girls were waitresses and that around Slane.
He had taken over the farm, but after he died his wife couldn't
manage it. She expected the children to work for nothing; if
ever they asked her for money she would say, 'The land will be
yours when I'm gone.' That wasn't any good to anyone, was it?
'Live horse and you'll get grass,' as Da used to say. So they all
up and left, one by one, and the last time I saw her she was an
old woman trying to drag in enough hay to feed the animals.
The farm's sold now – all gone.

It was not a very grand house, but the Kearneys, my father's
side of the family, did have a very grand house, a gentleman
farmer's house, down in Rosybrook in County Louth. They
still have it, and we had a holiday in it not long back. Our
family were not peasants – they were well-to-do farmers both
sides.

All I remember about my mother's mother was that she used
to go into a room on the farm at Rathmaiden, and shut herself
up to pray. We used to say to her, 'What do you go in there
and shut yourself up to pray for, Grannie?' And she would say,
'Because when I'm dead, none of you will pray for me!' My
grandfather used to carry me on his back. I was only a very
little child when he died. People say I'm like him.

It was a fairly big farm – I believe about a hundred acres.
There were plenty of animals – about twenty cows and five or
six horses. One of the horses saved my brother John's life. The
child ran out under the horse – but the animal bent down and
picked John up with his teeth and laid him to one side, before
pulling the cart on. Aren't horses mountains of sense? More
sense than humans . . . My brother lived to be over ninety.

Look how comfortable they were, and yet they lost all. How
did they lose it? Well, they set my father up with his shops and
houses. They gave him enough money to build a fine big house
at 68 Lower Dorset Street. He took my mother as a bride into
it. There's a plaque on the door now, put up by the
Corporation to my brother Peadar Kearney, who was born

there. In later years he became the poet of the revolution. He inspired the Republican Rebellion with his soldiers' song, which then became our National Anthem.

Mother and Father didn't drink or smoke, but they had a lot of children. Father had to find enough to send his six brothers and one sister off to America to seek their fortunes. He ran a grocer's shop and an off-licence, and he built a row of cottages alongside the pub. So at the start of their married life my parents were very well off, but then they lost all they had.

I heard from older members of the family that Father, instead of minding his businesses, used to go off to see what was happening in the courts. He began by taking just a passing interest in the law – you know the way farmers are, some of them will dispute over a blade of grass. Well, he was always disputing over everything. At first he went to the courts just to pass the time; then, like everything else, it went too far. He thought he was a judge, and used to spend all his day there in the law courts. He would dress up in a swallow-tail coat, white gloves and a tall black hat.

He left Mother in charge of the shops, and people would come from all parts of Dublin, saying to her, 'Mrs Kearney, me husband is out of work and me children are starving,' and she would give them anything out of the shop. Between that, and their relations robbing them when Mother's back was turned, the shops went. Once the houses and the shops were gone, my father was finished. He died very quickly of a broken heart. He thought he was a grand gentleman, but he died in one room, a terrible old room in a tenement house in Sean MacDermott Street.

I never lived at Dorset Street. My brother Patrick and I were born after the family moved to Dolphin's Barn. We were twins, and they made up a poem about us:

> Kathleen and Patrick were their names,
> They were twins and looked the same,
> They lived in Dolphin's Barn Lane,
> And Kathleen and Patrick were their names.

It's not called Dolphin's Barn Lane now, it's Dolphin's Barn Street, but Father's shop is still there. Although it's a fairly big shop, it was a come-down to him to go to the Barn. He couldn't get on in the business at all; he took a job in insurance, with the Royal Liver. When he died he told Mother, 'I could have done better,' and, poor woman, all she said was, 'Well, we saw the two days, one wet, one fine.' I think it was losing his shops that killed him, that and want, and trying to manage.

He died in 1894. At that time, if people were out of work, there wasn't a penny to be had. And when he died, he left six children, with the youngest two years old. There wasn't a penny at all, good, bad or indifferent, and Mother had to depend on her brother. When he came into Dublin with cows and hay, he would bring Mother a week's provisions for us, from his home in the country – her original home.

So my father, who was a rich man and then became a poor one, sentenced himself in the end with his law cases – and he sentenced the rest of us to the poor house. He never went mad – he was very intelligent. He taught us all the national songs, and when my sister brought her school books home the first thing he did was rip out the picture of Queen Victoria.

You might say he lost the shops and the houses through carelessness.

My mother could not manage, and in the end my sisters and I had to go into an orphanage. Mother explained to us that we had to go away. She just told us that she was sending us to a convent, where the nuns would be so kind, and everything would be lovely. I said nothing – I was only a child. I thought it might be for a day or two – I never dreamed it would be for so long. Like Ruth in the Bible: seven long years in exile.

I went into the orphanage on 29 March 1898 – a dull cold day to go into a dull cold place. But I got used to it. Indeed, some of the girls that were there all their young lives cried when the time came for them to go. The nuns were fairly strict with us, but they gave us enough to eat and drink. They never took us out – I never saw the outside from the day I went in to the day I came out. A very poor, plain yard, that's all we had – there were lovely meadows all round, and they never let us into them. Just the old yard and no meadows; that and plain food was my life for all those years. Still, I lived to tell the tale.

I was in the orphanage longer than my sisters. Baby was in for four years, then she went out dressmaking for half a crown a week. Maggie was only a year and a half in it. I was in the longest, because I was the youngest.

It was a religious place, the orphanage: Mass every morning, and then, during Lent, Benediction every night. Ridiculous – getting little children out of bed at six in the morning for Mass, and then into work sewing or cleaning or cooking, some of them in the laundry ironing. We did all the clothes, sheets and stuff for all the other religious houses; we baked our own bread, even mended our own shoes. They were learning us to be independent, to face the trials that lay ahead.

It was a fine training – after it you could live off the skin of a rasher. I didn't see meat for breakfast all the years I was in there. We had brown bread and some dripping, a mug of tea and that was it. For dinner you would get a thin slice of meat, just the odd one; but on the other hand, illness was unknown. We used to get up at six, then an hour's work in the dormitories, then an hour's Mass at seven; then we would work till twelve, then have a play in the dirty old yard, then back to work again. In summer we went to bed at eight, in winter at six. The orphanage was in Golden Bridge Road, Inchihore; I could look down out of my window on to the lights of Dublin. Many's the night I cried myself to sleep.

But you could never be lonely among a lot of children, and parents could come and visit us when the end of the month came. One day when Mother came the Mother Superior put half a crown into her hand. Our mother cried and showed me. I turned away – I couldn't bear to see her so grateful, she that had been so proud. When they were wed, Father had strewn flowers in her path from the farm to the chapel – poor Mother, to have come so low to be like a gipsy!

It wasn't all work in the orphanage. I never worried about what I would make of my life – all I thought of was reading. I used to read from morning to night. I'd even get up and read by the Sacred Heart lamp, which was very wrong. I nearly blinded myself. All I had to read was the holy books, and the stuff from the Catholic Truth Society of Ireland – the *Messenger* and *St Anthony's Annals*. The nuns taught us to act and sing. I still have some of the songs that the nuns taught us. One of them was 'What Are the Wild Waves Saying?' It's a duet – I couldn't sing the whole of it:

> What are the wild waves saying,
> Sister, the whole day long?
> That ever amid their praying
> I hear but a low loud song.
>
> Not by the sea-side only,
> There it sounds wild and free,
> But at night when it's dark and lonely,
> In dreams it is still with me.
>
> Brother, I hear no singing;
> 'Tis but the rolling waves.
> Ever the great wind blowing
> Over the ocean wave.

I used to sing that over eighty years ago.

I had a great friend in the orphanage; she lived at Phibsboro, up near Glasnevin cemetery. She grew up to be an awfully unlucky woman. Her husband was eaten alive by rats after a feed of drink. He went on the batter, and fell down in a ditch, and that was the end of him.

His poor head was all eaten away.

I had another friend, Chrissie, and her husband used to drink – he would drink Lough Eireann dry. She lost her two children, one from measles and the other from meningitis. Well – not saying one thing and thinking another – her husband came in one day to see her going out.

'Where are you going?' says he.

'Out to the pub.'

'But you don't drink.'

She looked at him. 'I do now. There's nothing to stop in for.'

And she drank him out of house and home. She ended up in a madhouse – she was caught up in the trees, jumping about like a monkey. She was a good mother – none better – but her husband drove her to it. Yet after it, he never drank – at least it cured *him*. He went religious, and wore his knees out praying – an oul craw thumper, God forgive me. Strange, isn't it, what happens to people?

As I mentioned, my sister Maggie was only in the orphanage for a year and a half, but she cried when she was taken out. They put her out to work. She was a dressmaker, and built up her company into that great business they have now. She was a great woman – didn't she rear a family as extraordinary as my own? Her son Kevin comes nearly every Sunday to see me; he's better to me than my own sons. Eamonn Andrews is married to a granddaughter of Maggie's, Grainne.

After I left the orphanage in 1904 I lived with Mother and Maggie and Baby in a tenement house in Sean MacDermott Street. It was just one room, but we were very happy. On a Sunday afternoon we would have our tea – maybe a currant bun, and we thought we had Heaven. I was a big mope of sixteen, and the others hid everything from me. I knew nothing, nothing at all about the facts of life. I thought that if you lay beside a man you had a baby.

Maggie got married at eighteen, and at her house, when I came into the room, they hid the baby clothes. But the next day I met a friend, Lily Ryan, and she told me all about it. I shouted at her, 'Lily Ryan, that's a terrible sin on your soul, you'll go to Hell for telling me such awful lies! You'll have to go to confession and tell the priest!' Can you imagine it – and me seventeen!

Well, the following night, I saw them hiding the baby clothes again, so I told them what Lily Ryan had told me. Well, they blushed scarlet, and what they didn't say to Lily . . .

The next morning she met me, and shouted, 'Ah, you, Kathleen Kearney, don't pretend I was the one to tell you about babies! Sure, you know more than any of us, and you're not letting on.'

There was a fellow called Paddy Curry in Slane who used to be courting me on my holidays there. We thought all we had to do was go into Drogheda to be married – but someone came after us and brought us back. We had no sense – we were only seventeen. I wasn't in love with him, indeed I wasn't, and he would not have been bothered with me at all, only there were no girls living there. He got married after; he's dead now.

It was some years later that I met Jack Furlong.

2

First Marriage and Easter Rising

'Ireland forever held their graves'

Kathleen married her first husband, Jack Furlong, a fellow Republican, during the First World War. Both Kathleen and Jack were actively involved in the Easter Rising (the Rebellion) in 1916, and Kathleen met some of its greatest heroes, including the charismatic Michael Collins, whom she greatly admired in spite of her detestation of his subsequent Free State policy for Ireland. In 1918 Jack died suddenly, leaving Kathleen with one small son, Rory, and another, Sean still to be born

It was in 1915 that I was introduced to Jack by my brother Peadar. He came to a dance we were holding in aid of the Cummann ne Mban, the women's movement of the IRA. He was a grand dancer and I took to him from the start. He couldn't put two words together to save his life – awfully shy but willing enough, poor soul. I was determined to have him. I was going out at the time with Paddy Donnelly, a fella who had worked as an assistant in one of my father's shops. I liked the cut of Jack Furlong and he had a good steady job at that time: he was a printer's compositor. He was a member of the Irish Volunteers with my brother Peadar and so with the Republican Movement – and that meant we had everything in common.

He was a very saintly man. He never missed saying the rosary from the night we were married to the night he died. But, as I said, he was one of the rebels – his name is over the door of Jacob's Garrison.* His mother sewed uniforms for the lads in 1916.

When we were married we were both very innocent about the sex business, though we found out soon enough, and had two sons. I never knew there was such a thing as a contraceptive until my sons were grown and I found one under a pillow once. I suppose I must have burned it. I knew nothing about the homosexual business either, and my sister Maggie died without knowing anything about it. If you said the word to her

*Jacob's biscuit factory was one of the strongholds of the rebels during Easter Week (*Ed.*)

37

she would say, 'What's that?' We were reared very foolish.

Here's a thing you'd hardly believe. Jack Furlong was in work – he had a grand job at MacDaw's the printers – but I decided to try and get a job. It would be a bit of extra money, and I was sick of stopping at home and doing nothing. I went to see this young gentleman about a job, and we were walking along talking about it. It was a summer's day and the sun was splitting the trees. I was three months pregnant with Rory – though I didn't tell him that – and I got very tired.

'Well, sit down for a bit,' he said, and we sat down on the sward. Didn't he start into me – pulling and tugging at my blouse, trying to drag my dress down? I nearly died.

'Take your hands off me! Don't you dare attack me – I'm a married woman!' I said as he tore the belt off my dress.

He said, 'I was only going to kiss you.'

I said, 'You wouldn't have any right to kiss me! I am a married woman. I told you that.'

But he wouldn't let go.

I had an idea. 'Let me stand up,' I said. 'Just let me stand up and I will let you, if you just let me stand up . . .' And he did. As I ran down to the city with him looking after me I was crying, 'Look, you could take my life, you could kill me now, but you'll never do *that* with me!' That was the only attempt that was ever made on me.

I never told either of my husbands about that, because they might think I led the man on. I wouldn't have, though, because I never enjoyed the sex business very much. I thought it would be vulgar. I would pretend to be enjoying it, but I would really be adding up my debts for the next day. I loved having children, though. If I were a young woman again and could use contraceptives, I wouldn't, because the happiest days of my life were when the children were young all around me.

Soon after we were married came the Rebellion. I remember that Easter Monday: the weather was great. You could have fried a rasher on the ground. The fighting began at noon. I was given messages to carry: the very first was to Pearse and Connolly,* who were occupying the Post Office.

The GPO was a very grand building in Sackville Street. Across the street was Nelson's Pillar, sign of British domination. (I was so glad when they blew that pillar up in the 1960s. I never thought it would go in my lifetime!) I took my dispatch to the leaders of the Rebellion, and I must say they didn't look like the heroes they really were. Connolly was a little fat man with a great big moustache; Pearse was wall-eyed, God bless the mark! I had met him before at a *ceilidh*. He was a lovely, handsome man, and was known then as the leader of the movement. (They say now he was one of the 'queer fellas', but people are so dirty-minded; they say more than their prayers.) He didn't speak much to the likes of me – too busy.

The men of my family and my husband were all in Jacob's biscuit factory in Wexford Street: Jacob's Garrison we called it. The Volunteers had taken it and defended it all the week.

You must remember, though, that some half of the family were off to fight for the British in the First World War. Jim Behan, the brother of my second husband, was killed in the front line on the Somme. His name is on the Arches to the Fallen at St Stephen's Green. My son Seamus is called after him. Jack Furlong's brother Harry was in the British Army, too. Every house had a son serving in the British Army, so there were many against the Rebellion. In some ways Dublin had done well out of the war. The war meant money for those who might not have had work without it, and the Irish had always supplied the British Army's horses.

So there was no mass support for us. A crowd gathered around Jacob's, shouting, 'If you want to fight, go to France!' Dublin was divided over the Rebellion. One friend of mine, Mrs Slater, lost three sons in it – and she wasn't a rebel at all.

But some of the men who'd joined the British Army were for us, and gave information about what their plans were. It was

*Padraic Pearse was a leader of the Irish Volunteers (subsequently called the IRA) in Easter Week, and proclaimed the Irish Republic as a sovereign state. James Connolly was the founder of the Republican Party and Irish Citizen Army (*Ed.*)

from one of them that we learned that the British planned to shell the buildings we had taken. No one had thought that the British would destroy their own property – that was why the plan was to take and occupy large buildings, rather than fight in the streets. Our aim was always to defend, rather than attack.

Down at St Stephen's Green the great Countess Markievicz was showing that women can hold their ground, too. She was a member of the Irish Citizen Army – the armed section of the trade unions – although she was one of the upper classes. She was born a Gore-Booth, and became the greatest horsewoman in Ireland. She learned her courage on the hunting field, going over the very wildest fences with the men trotting after. Don't forget that they rode side-saddle in those days.

Anyway, as soon as the Rebellion started she was out there in her uniform – which consisted of an immense floppy hat and a green tunic and skirt. It was supposed to be based on the uniform of the Boers when they fought the British in South Africa. She started to dig a hole in St Stephen's Green, to defend it against assault by the Brits.

Now, although there was all this fighting going on, many people were trying their best to ignore it and go on working as usual. Near her dug-out were some men working on scaffolding, and they started to jeer at this mad woman in uniform digging a hole in the middle of a park. In the end she couldn't stand it any longer, and loosed off at them with her pistol, which she carried with her. They didn't stay at work after that.

Most of the leaders of the 1916 Rebellion were holy men. Patrick Pearse was next door to being a spoiled priest. But not Michael Collins – the big fella, as we used to call him, though he wasn't that big, just about five feet ten inches. But he was broad as he was long. I can see him now sitting with his long legs swinging on the edge of a desk and his eyes smiling. I always thought he had very lustful lips. A woman's man, which Pearse wasn't. Collins was sent to be one of the very high-ups in the Rebellion. But he was the bravest of the brave. He led a charge of rebels through the British lines and the only thing that hit him out of a hail of bullets was a burning bit of a door. He had his coat scorched and that was all.

When I met him he was in charge of a thing, I think it was called National Aid. It was before the White Cross, though it helped the dependants of Republican prisoners and the cause itself. He got millions out of the Americans. The thing about him was he wouldn't touch a penny for himself, and every last farthing had to be accounted for.

He left there about 1920 and became General Collins in the War of Independence. I think he won the war for us. Because he was down to earth and not a saint in Heaven, he could see that the one thing that had crippled every rebellion in the past was the paid informer. Even though the very name 'informer' could blacken a family in Ireland, for ten generations the British had still recruited them. In any case they had six hundred years of Dublin Castle intelligence behind them. Collins decided that if the British were to be beaten then he would have to put out their 'eyes', as he called them, and block their 'ears'.

He started by getting people in the heart of the enemy Dublin Castle to inform him who the informers were. Now he was a humane man, and every informer would get a letter saying, 'There is a boat leaving Dublin tomorrow morning at seven. In the interest of you and your family, be on it.' His men in the Castle kept him informed of the movements of the British before they knew themselves. It's true he shot a lot of intelligence officers in Mount Street one night. Da knew, but never spoke to me about it. All he would say was that it was a terrible thing to walk into a hotel room and shoot a man dead beside his wife or mistress.

Collins himself had an enormous price on his head, alive or dead. Even so, one day he was walking down a street when he met an armed patrol. The corporal shouted out, 'What's your name then, Paddy?'

Collins laughed and shouted, 'How about Mick Collins?'

The corporal pushed a gun into Collins's head and smiled. 'I wish it was, me old Pat, I would be two hundred pounds the richer tonight.'

It was really Collins who beat the British out of Southern Ireland. Even though they had tens of thousands of troops, by 1921 he had beaten them hollow. He organized the counter-terror in the Black and Tan war.* I heard him say, 'If they shoot one of ours, burn down the richest man's house in the neighbourhood and tell them why.'

You know, I have always regarded the pub as the poor man's club. There is nothing nicer than a pub, yet some of the holy men frowned on the pubs. But not Collins. He knew everyone went to a pub, Irish or English, so he used the pubs as the centre of his operations. He used to go into a pub and just look at the bar. The drinks in front of certain barmen in a corner of the pub told him everything: sherry for intelligence officers, wine for the G men of the police, and plain port for military police.

He had the British running round in circles until finally, as the world knows, he signed the Treaty ending the War of Independence and creating our first Free State. He was killed by our own in the Civil War, on 22 August 1922. The Irish assassin's bullet – probably that of an old comrade in arms – did for Collins what the might of the British Army never could.

Anyway, back to 1916. The British crushed our Rebellion easily enough – after all, they had thirty thousand to our six hundred. They even brought a gunboat up the River Liffey and beat the heart out of the city. It was a sad sight to see the captured rebels, some led in chains down to the boats bound

*This was the War of Independence, fought against the British (the Black and Tans) after the unilateral declaration in 1919 of a provisional government for a new Irish Republic. The war was ended by the signing of the Treaty in 1921 which created the Irish Free State, but its terms were too much of a compromise for the Republicans and resulted in the Civil War, fought between the Free Staters, led by Michael Collins, who had signed the Treaty, and the Anti Free Staters, led by Eamonn De Valera (*Ed.*)

for the prison camps in England. The others – our leaders – well, they were for something else. A death party. Most of them could not believe that brave men taken in battle would be shot like mad dogs, but they were, and even though their bodies were burned in quicklime, Ireland forever held their graves.

Nothing could wipe out the feeling that most of us had when we heard the news. The very announcement of the death list was really the end for the British in Ireland, even though we did not know it then. Really, you know, the people couldn't stand it, and when they heard that James Connolly was strapped to a wheelchair and then shot, it maddened them – so much so that the very people that spat on the rebels as they were dragged to the ships now queued up to join the War of Independence.

It was strange, the rebel leaders *were* like holy men. They died like saints. They had kept faith with the Republican ideal, and in an act of madness went out again to affirm that Irishmen would not be part of the Empire. Our rebels were defeated, but in the manner of their going they snatched victory from the jaws of defeat.

I could have been happy all my life with Jack, but we were married for less than three years. He died in the great influenza epidemic of 1918. That was the biggest epidemic the world has ever known – it was spread all over the world by soldiers returning from the Great War in France. A terrible thing – I believe more died of the influenza than died in the war itself. In Dublin, one died in every house, and my Jack died in my house.

3

The Civil War

'Men don't marry women – it's the women that marry the men'

After four years of widowhood Kathleen met and married Stephen Behan in 1922. Politics – this time the Civil War – were in the forefront of this second marriage, too, and very soon Kathleen found herself living in a slum tenement with her children while Stephen was a prisoner of the Free Staters. There were to be five children from this marriage: four boys, Brendan, Seamus, Dominic and Brian, plus another son who died young, Fintan, and one girl, Carmel

So I was left a widow with one son, Rory, and carrying another, Sean, who was born six months after Jack died. I had by now no mother of my own to help me, but I did have my mother-in-law, Mrs Furlong. She was a remarkable woman, a rebel all her life. She lived down in Great Charles Street – it was in the basement there that she sewed the uniforms for the rebels of Easter Week. She and her husband were always in the I R A. When her husband died, she wanted to leave Dublin, and 'the boys', as we call them, got her a house in England, where she took in those that were making ammunition and so on. Running a house for I R A men on the run – that just suited her. But then one day the house caught fire – somebody was careless with the explosive, I suppose – and she was sent to jail. Imagine that – an old woman, nearer eighty than seventy, jailed for running a 'bombing house'!

After Sean was born, then, I went out to look for work while Mrs Furlong minded the boys. Madame Markievicz, the Countess that defended St Stephen's Green in 1916, got a job for me. (Didn't we have a lot of gentry on our side?) I went to her because I knew she would help a poor woman with children to support, and she did. She asked Madame Mac-Bride, widow of Major John MacBride that was executed in 1916, to find me a job in her house at St Stephen's Green. It wasn't a bad job, though Madame MacBride paid very little (my meals and that and a little money besides), but then I wasn't really a servant – more a receptionist. I let the visitors in

47

and answered the telephone. Didn't you say that's what Joyce
called Ireland – the servant at the door? So, although I got very
little for it, I didn't feel degraded ever, and that was worth
something.

One person I don't remember ever letting into the house at
St Stephen's Green was a policeman. Madame MacBride was
in fact living in Ireland illegally – I'll tell you about that in a
moment – but the British authorities didn't seem to bother her
once she was in. Maybe they had the sense to see we'd win
anyway, with her or without her.

I'd better explain about this 'Madame' business, too. As I
said, we had a lot of gentry on our side – the Nationalist side –
and they didn't want to use English expressions like Mr and
Mrs. On the other hand, if they'd used the Gaelic version,
'Mrs MacBride' would come out as 'Ban MacBride', which
means 'MacBride's woman'. And that wouldn't do for them –
they thought it was common. So all these grand Irish ladies
were Madame this and Madame that, as though they were
French. The working classes didn't bother with such nonsense
– Mrs Furlong or Mrs Behan was good enough for me.

Even before Major MacBride had been executed for his part
in the Rebellion he and his wife had been separated for some
time. I'm not sure if they were ever divorced. Maybe that was
what sent him out in 1916 – you wouldn't know what drives
people, would you? Certainly it was a strange thing – he
had fought out in Africa for the Boers, during the Boer War.
They say he was the only one of the Easter Week leaders who'd
ever seen a shot fired in anger before. I never knew him, of
course.

Madame MacBride was a beautiful woman. She had been an
actress at the Abbey Theatre – she was the first that played the
Countess Cathleen in Yeats's play of that name. In fact, not
long before I went to St Stephen's Green she'd evicted Yeats
and his wife from her house. She had been living in France –
she was banned from coming to Ireland because of her part in
the Rebellion – and she'd rented them the house. But now
she'd found a way to come back secretly, disguised as a beggar

woman. Yeats's wife was sick with the influenza, and he refused
to let Madame MacBride into her own house, in case she'd upset
her. Later, though, Madame MacBride got her way.

In fact Yeats had another reason not to want the two of them
in the house together. It was no secret that he'd been in love
with Madame MacBride for years. He loved her for her beauty
– as a woman to write poems about – and hated her being
mixed up with politics and standing up on a cart to address the
crowd, although of course he was for a free Ireland himself. It's
all in his poems:

> Have I not seen the loveliest woman born
> Out of the mouth of Plenty's horn,
> Because of her opinionated mind
> Barter that horn and every good
> By quiet natures understood
> For an old bellows full of angry wind?

He thought she'd been ruined by taking up politics – she
should just have stopped at home and looked beautiful. Isn't
that like a man? She did a lot more good the way she was. She
led the women in Easter Week, with her Sam Browne belt and
a great big hat – a pistol and all. And before that, in the strike
of 1913, she would be down among the poor cooking for them,
with a great big apron on.

Not that these great Nationalist ladies ever forgot their place
in life. Madame Markievicz, in particular, thought she was
very grand; her manner was very sour. Mrs Tom Clarke told
me that when the three of them (her, Madame MacBride and
Madame Markievicz) were in prison, the two Madames spent
all their time talking about their 'blood' – the noble blood in
their veins – and she was just the poor woman. Though her
husband had been shot, he was only a shop-keeper, so she was
no one. 'Merciful Heavens,' I said to Mrs Clarke, 'and these
were our leaders!'

Anyway, Madame MacBride was a match for William Yeats
– 'Silly Willie', she used to call him – and was mistress in her

own house when I arrived. I had a busy time as her receptionist. She was often giving parties or holding meetings in the evening, and during the day there would be people calling on her, to ask her help or just to keep in with her. They had to be careful, though, as she could be a tartar. They say that James Joyce hardly ever dared call on her, for fear of what she'd say about his clothes, which were always shabby.

Joyce had left Dublin for good by then, and gone to live on the Continent, but he'd been a familiar face around Dublin before he went away. Everyone knew everyone else in Dublin in those days – it was just the right size for a city. Joyce had a beautiful singing voice, and many said he could have done well as a singer if he hadn't wanted to write books. His family lived very near mine, on the North Circular Road, and we were quite similar in many ways. Just like mine, they'd gone from riches to poverty.

I did meet Joyce's wife, but only briefly. It was during the Civil War and she was up to her eyes in muck and bullets, as the saying goes. She was nearly done for on a train to Galway, with bullets flying over her head. 'A funny-looking woman,' Da once said. 'Nora Barnacle by name and nature. Joyce can be sure of one thing – she will stick to him through Hell or high water.'

Nora told me terrible things about Joyce. Sure the man was crackers all for free love and yet he wanted his poor wife to do the dog on him to beat what else, to bestride him like Molly and whip him till he howled. Did you ever hear the likes of it, sure the man was crackers! I told her not to worry. But I need not have bothered – she was country, one beef to the heel like a Mullingar heifer. He didn't bother *her*. *She* thought he was potty. The lazy woman never washed a cup in her natural. Joyce took himself all too seriously – all that talk about being our conscience! He only wanted to leave his family, but he ran straight into another. She was supposed to be in a peculiar condition before he left Ireland with her. I wonder, was she, or did she make it all up? We will never know now, will we?

★

I was four years a widow. After a while I left Madame MacBride's house and got a job with the Dublin Corporation. The money was much better – five pounds a week. That was more than my Jack had been getting as a compositor. As a widow I could do whatever I liked – but then I met Stephen Behan.

Stephen was a foreman house-painter and decorator, the very best tradesman in Dublin. For fifteen years he was President of the Painters' Union. He was a great friend of my brother Peadar; they were both painters, and they used to meet at the pub – at the 'circle'. But I first met him through Mrs Furlong. He'd known Jack from attending Gaelic language classes – they were great butties – and after Jack died he went on coming to Mrs Furlong's house for parties. I loved him the very first time I saw him. Men don't marry women, you know, it's the women that marry the men – and we were married in no time.

Living at Mrs Furlong's then, along with me and my two sons, was my brother-in-law, Harry Furlong. As I've said, he'd fought with the British Army during the First World War, and the gassing, bombing and shooting had sent him dotty. He didn't go roaring mad or anything, but he started acting strange. Harry helped look after the children while I was at work. He was a very handsome fellow, and I was very fond of him. But all I had for him were the feelings of a sister. The only men I ever fancied in *that* way were my two husbands – certainly never Harry. But one day suddenly he asked me to marry him. I was due to marry Stephen in three weeks: 'Forget him,' Harry said. 'He's a drunkard – you should marry me!'

I was horrified and ran away from him. Later, Harry married a young woman who thought I had lived with him, and called me all sorts of terrible names, including 'prostitute'. But it wasn't true. Harry never even kissed me.

I married that 'drunkard' Stephen, and soon was expecting a baby – Brendan. But trouble also came quickly. We'd been married perhaps two months when Stephen was arrested. It was 1922, and Ireland was in a state of civil war. It wasn't the

British that had got him but our own people – those that were for the Free State. We called them the Murder Gang.

At that time we were living in a flat in Inchihore. I was doing the washing – rubbing his overalls on an old scrubbing board – when somebody knocked on the door. He had a letter in his hand, but he wasn't the postman. 'Kathleen Behan? This is for you – I found it in the street.'

It tells you something about those times that you could do that – just drop a letter and be sure someone would see it delivered. All it said was, 'I've been arrested, but I will be home soon. Stephen.' In fact he was away for two years. He was sent to Kilmainham, a prison for IRA men in Dublin. Here I was, paying a fabulous rent for this flat in Inchihore, and no money coming in all of a sudden. There was no help for it – I had to go to Stephen's mother.

Both my mothers-in-law were extraordinary women, but that was all they had in common. Mrs Furlong was always good to me, but Stephen's Ma – the Grannie, as we called her – didn't like me one bit. When I was first married to her son, I'd told her, as one woman to another, about the young man who'd tried to rape me when I was looking for a job. That was a mistake – all she said was that I must have encouraged him. She was mad at me for marrying Stephen – I don't know why, because I don't think he ever gave her any money. She was a lovely, handsome woman – black hair down to her waist at the age of eighty-four – and she thought me ugly. I heard her say once, 'When that ugly wan could get two husbands, surely a plain wan could get one!' Stephen had no love for his mother at all; but now, when he was in prison, she said at once, 'Kathleen, come and live with me.' That was generous, but in other ways she was mean. I recall Stephen saying, 'She could live where another person would die.'

I remember looking down over the terrible broken-down tenement houses of Russell Street, where she lived, and saying to my sister-in-law Chrissie, 'Do you think I could ever live in one of those?' Well, in the end I had to live in one of those dirty old houses, and be grateful, because the Grannie owned them all. What else could I do?

I didn't actually live with her, but in an apartment in one of the tenements. At first we had just one room, and it was no thanks to my mother-in-law that we had even that. Though she was keen enough for us to live with her, she didn't want us taking up rooms that she could get money for. So to begin with we had to make do with whatever space we could find. There was a lady in the basement who'd come down in life – she had lived in Rathmines, which was very posh then – and she was just about to move out, so she gave me the key to her room. I was settling the children there when this country girl turned up. 'This room was promised to me,' she said.

I'm quiet enough until I'm roused, but I'd had enough without this one grabbing my room. 'I'll break your face if you don't leave me alone, you impudent get out of Hell!' It was all the Grannie's fault – she'd let the room without telling me – but I wouldn't yield. You have to look after yourself or you never get anywhere. The girl wouldn't go, so I chased her with a sweeping brush, crying, 'What I have I hold!'

When the Grannie came round in the morning, there we were living in the basement, and there was nothing she could do about it. Later, we got a kitchen in much the same way, but in the fourteen years we lived there that was the most we had – just those two rooms. My sons had to sleep six to a bed – three at the top and three at the tail.

Brendan was born while his father was still in prison. It's hard for the young women to believe this now, but if you had a child in hospital in those days you had to pay up on the nail, or they'd try and stop you leaving. I heard of a woman in the Rotunda (a big maternity hospital) who told the doctors she couldn't pay. She had no money. 'Well,' they said, 'you can just stay here until somebody comes to pay for you.' She stopped there two days or more, but of course nobody came with the money, so in the end they had to put her out. You weren't treated well.

I remember taking Brendan down to Kilmainham as a baby in my arms, and holding him up to the cell window for his father to see. Stephen waved down at us – but we never went inside. The Civil War was a terrible time to be alive. We'd thought all we had to do was get rid of the Brits, and we'd all be on the pig's back. But here were our own people being as bad – or worse. When the Dail voted for the Treaty,* which would put Ireland in the British Empire, some of the lads made an Irish flag with the Union Jack in the corner and hoisted it over the GPO, to remind us all of 1916. That's what the Treaty meant – the end of the Irish Republic. Now it was the Free State army that we had to fight, and they were worse than the Black and Tans.

I hated the Free Staters – they shot seventy-seven patriots. 'Remember the Seventy-seven!' was our war cry for years. They shot more in a day than the British did in twenty years. They even shelled the Four Courts in Dublin, with Rory O'Connor's men inside. The Courts were the Republican headquarters. The British blew the centre of the city out in 1916 – the Free State finished it off in 1922.

Two wars in five years! It was brother against brother, and families divided. I heard terrible stories. At one time the Free Staters strapped live IRA prisoners to the front of their armoured cars, so that if they hit a landmine they'd go up first. No wonder Sean O'Casey said we should put love in our hearts and take out murderous hate. Was there ever a nation with such a spiteful face towards each other as ours? Our biggest industries are undertakers and glaziers.

I blame the British – divide and rule, divide and conquer, was their policy even when they left after the Treaty. It was awful that the Free Staters used the old British Army barracks, the old British Army uniforms, rifles, everything. Mind you, they had a hard job getting people to join up. They had to lift the pay to three pounds ten a week: that was good money then. A tradesman would be hard set to earn two. Even then, the Free Staters only recruited the sweepings off the street.

*The Treaty made Ireland the Irish Free State, a Dominion of the British Empire, and gave the North the option to secede. This was unacceptable to the Republican movement (*Ed.*)

I remember going down to Slane to visit my relations, and the IRA boys were firing from the hedges right across the train. Merciful hour, I nearly died, with machine gun bullets ripping across us! I caught Brendan and held him tight. We had to lie flat under the old wooden benches they had in the trains in them days, while over our heads the madmen fought it out. You see, we had some Free Stater troops on the train, supposed to be guarding us. I thought we would have been a lot better off without them.

When I came back to Dublin I went through O'Connell Street, or Sackville Street as it was called then, and the heart, liver and lights were torn out of the city. You wouldn't know it! Half of Dublin was in ruins. They were shelling the Four Courts as well – or was that after? I can't be sure. You forget, you know, when you're old. But one thing I am sure of – whatever the British began, we finished off. I was told that in the Phoenix Park they found dismembered corpses with their hair, teeth and tongues pulled out. Sure, savages in the jungle wouldn't behave any worse, would they? Brendan had a nice one about the Civil War. 'Civil War!' says he. 'Bedad, if this is what a civil war looked like, I would hate to see an uncivil one.'

Though he'd signed the Treaty, and I hated it, I was heartbroken when the news came over the radio that that lovely man Mick Collins had been shot in an ambush. To be killed by Irishmen after half a lifetime escaping execution by the British! He'd helped us when I was first widowed – the IRA was a sort of unofficial welfare state for poor Republicans, and Mick saw to that side of it. My brother Peadar went to see him in jail, saying, 'Mick, me sister's husband has just died, and she's in very poor circumstances.'

'Well,' says he, 'all I have here is twenty pounds, Peadar, but take it and give it to your sister.'

In a way Collins's death left me sadder than the executions of 1916. At least those men died to give us hope.

When the news of his death reached them, the very

Republican prisoners kept in jail by Collins knelt down in thousands to recite the rosary for a light that was gone forever. It was his own bravery did for him, as well. In the ambush he refused to allow the armoured cars to drive on, but told them to stop and fight. That was where he was wrong: treachery was even within his own ranks. One of the armoured car drivers had betrayed him, and complained that the machine gun had jammed when it hadn't. Collins was shot in Beal na Blath, the Valley of the Flowers, in Cork. He thought he would be safe amongst his own people. The Collins family came from Cork, and he had said sadly before going there: 'Surely they won't shoot one of their own?' But they did.

Wasn't it a terrible thing to slaughter the nearest leader we had to Napoleon?

4

Russell Street

'They called me Lady Behan'

Kathleen, Stephen and their ever-increasing family spent fourteen years during the twenties and thirties in one of Stephen's mother's tenement houses in Russell Street, a place of great poverty but equal camaraderie. What the children lacked in material benefits they gained in other ways, for books and music, lively conversation and a strong sense of Irish cultural tradition were all readily available in the Behan household. In 1932 De Valera became prime minister, but the Republicans' joy at having their own man in a position of power quickly turned to bitter disappointment when they realized he was an empty theorist and could do nothing to aid the plight of the working people

I couldn't give in to misery for long with my children all around me. I loved to take them walking through the city. I was a nymph for fresh air – the children had to have the air, as I'd have died without it. I hardly ever took a tram, although they were very cheap. Maybe it was all those years stuck indoors at the orphanage, after spending so much time on the farm. And soon Stephen was out in the air, too – back home from Kilmainham – and I settled down to married life in the tenements of Russell Street.

We were desperately poor. When Stephen first came back he was a long time walking about looking for a job. They wouldn't let the ex-prisoners work – trying to starve us to death, I suppose. But for the Grannie we *would* have starved to death. She had a great old saying: 'To Hell with poverty, let's kill a chicken!' and many and many's the goose or fine fat turkey she slung into our kitchen – you could eat until your jaw dropped off. She might have been mean to others, but I can't think what we'd have done without her, for as it was I felt scourged with poverty. Then one day we had a visitor – one of my relations from America.

I told you how my father had six brothers and a sister that he had to pay fares to America for. One became a banker, and the sister became Mother Superior of a convent. But not all the American Kearneys were so respectable – not by the time of Prohibition in the 1920s.

This man was in the rackets – one of the bootleggers. Maybe

he saw himself as paying back what his side of the family owed mine, but it was a queer way to do it. It didn't take him long to tell us his proposition. He wanted Stephen and a few of his butties to go out to America and work for him. They were to guard his stores of booze and 'take care' of anyone who caused trouble. They'd all been gunmen in the IRA, after all, so they had (as he put it) 'experience in that line of work'. To my horror, Stephen and his friends said they'd consider it. It would be easy money, they reckoned, and maybe shooting people was a trade like any other. I'd have shown that man the door. When he'd gone I cried my eyes out. 'You'll get killed,' I said, 'and then what will happen to us all?' Stephen laughed – he wasn't afraid of death. Neither was I, but I was afraid to see my children starve.

Then, just like a miracle, Dockerell's the builders offered Stephen a job. Even an IRA gunman would rather have steady work in his own trade than risk death in America, so he told the bootlegger, 'No.' After that, he was in constant work for many years. So that was a relief – not that we were ever rich in Russell Street.

What was Russell Street really like? You may well ask. Did you know that not a stone's throw from us was born Sean O'Casey, author of *The Plough and the Stars*? I think I've already mentioned that down the North Circular Road had lived James Joyce – he was in Richmond Terrace, a cul-de-sac he called the 'one-eyed street'. Have you read *Ulysses*? It's very high-class and all mixed up. The North Circular itself was a great wide street, built, according to Brendan, to move troops around a rebellious city and to give the soldiers a wide field of fire.

The houses in Russell Street were typical Dublin tenements with large windows. Some were shiny with clean curtains, others dusty and grimy, hiding dirty rags of curtains. Some of the houses were the 'closed hall door' kind. They were lived in by people who had work and could afford bigger rents. Ours was the other kind, with doors that hung back into the gloomy hallway day and night. The pub on the corner was then

Fannin's. It was later bought by Jemmy Gill, whose name it bears to this day.

The kids played football in the street before darkness fell, while the 'big fellows' stood around in scattered groups at both corners, some playing cards, others arguing how best the country should be governed.

'Collins effed it all up when he made the deal with Britain!'

'Yer an effing liar! Dev was the cause of it all. Everyone knows he betrayed when the British captured him – declared himself an effing Yank!'

The 'big fellows' were the men who couldn't or wouldn't find regular work. They lived by their wits, picking up five shillings here or there to increase – or more often to lose – it on the horse races. When they hadn't any money, they would stand on the corner beside Jemmy Gill's pub, waiting to see what the day's luck would bring. They could be coarse, and would fight and use bad language on a Saturday night. But they had the good rebel spirit all right.

Another din could be heard as the children of the Street followed the lamplighter. 'Billy with the lamp, Billy with the light, Billy with his sweetheart out all night,' they chanted as they followed him like the Pied Piper from lamp post to lamp post. At the pub corner was the newspaper man – short, stout, red-faced, with a ginger moustache twirled up at the corners army-style, a flat greasy cloth cap and a scarf knotted round his neck. *'N'Girrell! ... Hella Mail!'* he shouted. That meant *Evening Herald* and *Evening Mail*. You know, he had been a sergeant-major in the British Army. He was the one Englishman in *The Quare Fellow* – apart from the hangman.

And as for the Rustlers, as they called themselves – I'd never known people like those slum-dwellers of Russell Street. They called me Lady Behan, because I wouldn't sit on the steps gossiping all day as they did. They were as common as ditchwater, but in the things that really mattered they were the cream of the earth. They looked after each other in sickness, and for all their poverty they had a grand time. We used to sing and dance every opportunity we got. Yes, the slums were bad, but are the new housing estates any better? There the mothers sit in the pubs all day, and have no idea half the time where their children are. That's how you get this vandalism. The Russell Street children were bold lumps enough, but there was always someone on the Street keeping a watch on them.

Not that people didn't take a drink, you understand, and it was a rough place on a Saturday night – a drunken night. Then the people would get very drunk and use foul language – swearing at anything and everybody they came across. I didn't like it much, but I had to put up with it – I lived there. When they were drunk they'd forget 'Lady Behan' and call us 'Bloody old Fenians'.

Stephen didn't care. As long as he got his pint he didn't care. He was a good hard worker, never in bed after seven o'clock in the morning, and he liked the pub at night after working so hard all day. He loved his children, but he took no notice of them. I don't think he'd ever have got married at all if he hadn't met me.

He was almost trained as a priest. He started at the seminary, but his mother suddenly took him out without a word. She had the money all right, but she just wouldn't spend it on her son. He hated her for it – and he left the Church, saying he'd only darken its door again if they made him Pope. He wouldn't be one of the flock; he said a sheep had four legs but he had two, and no wool – he was bald.

I asked Da to go back to his religion a few times, but I just gave up in the end. He wouldn't listen to me at first, then he went to church once or twice, and then he gave it up for ever. He said he couldn't. No, he didn't like it at all. 'Kathleen,' he said, 'I can't endure it. My knees are worn out.'

He said he would go back to it when it had some sex in it. Did you ever hear such a thing? I said, 'Stephen, that's blasphemy!' He said he couldn't care less. I said I had enough of sex or maybe not enough. Da said the country was full of children but no sex.

I said to him one day, 'You must believe in something. Even a pig has a religion.' All he said back was that a pig ends up as sliced bacon. He wouldn't go to church, chapel or meeting houses. He would call on the children to get up and go out and meet their God on a Sunday morning, but he wouldn't stir himself, only turn over and go back to sleep again. He'd pretend he'd already been up and out to half six Mass, and had come home and gone back to bed again.

Even so, religion or no religion, he was a good man. He was very musical too. He used to sing light opera, and we used to sing duets together in the local pubs for we both loved singing. I must have been born happy and been born singing. I have danced my way through life. At home Da played the violin a lot for the kids. Here's a song he used to sing. I've sung it myself too, but Da did it beautifully. It's called 'What Will You Do, Love?'

What will you do, love, when I am going,
With white sail flowing, the seas beyond,
What will you do, love, when waves divide us,
And friends may chide us for being fond?

Tho' waves divide us and friends be chiding,
In faith abiding, I'll still be true,
And I'll pray for thee on the stormy ocean,
In deep devotion – that's what I'll do.

What would you do, love, when home returning,
With hopes high burning, with wealth for you,
If my barque which bounded o'er foreign foam,
Should be lost near home – ah! what would you do?

So thou wert spar'd, I'd bless the morrow,
In want and sorrow, that left me you!
And I'd welcome thee from the wasting billow,
This heart thy pillow – that's what I'd do!

I remember Da, Grannie and Brendan all had little hands and little feet. Brendan and the Grannie adored one another, but he never got on too well with his Da. I think maybe he was bitter that Da had not done more for him in the way of education. They were always rowing, but I think underneath it all they were very fond of each other in their own ways. The time when Brendan was wanted for the attempted shooting of a policeman, much later, it was Da who saved his life by getting an old friend to have the shoot-on-sight order lifted. It was at times like this when Da showed what he really felt for Brendan.

He wrote a piece about him, too. It's called 'The Golden Boy':

Brendan was a very good-looking child and was usually very even tempered. But he had another side. Because he was the golden boy, he always wanted his own way. There was a vicious streak in him side by side with the personality of a sensitive little boy. I remember finding him one day with a little boy half his size up against the railings and the child nearly throttled. We pulled him off, but Brendan still wanted a go at the child who had angered him. Another time I discovered that he had tortured a dog which had bitten him a few minutes before. He played a dastardly trick on one of our neighbours in Russell Street. He put sacks over the windows of her room so that when she woke up she thought she was blind. She didn't know whether it was night or day until someone opened the door three days later and let the light in. Brendan was also very jealous of any of the other children who managed to attract his Grannie's attention. He didn't want his position to be usurped. Once he discovered that Seamus (his younger brother) had scrounged a penny from the Grannie. Brendan rushed up the stairs, grabbed Seamus and threw him down shouting, 'She's my Grannie, not yours.'

Da had to suffer a lot for Brendan's faults. I remember Brendan spoke against Paddy Kavanagh, the poet, in a court action one time. Myself and Da met Paddy in a grand public house we used to go to, and I said to Da, 'As you pass Paddy Kavanagh only bow to him and say, "Good morning, Paddy."' Instead of that Da went right up to him and said, 'How are you, Paddy?' Well, Kavanagh started grunting like a stuck pig and just said, 'Kiss my arse'. He hated all us Behans on account of Brendan. He said once, 'That man Behan is evil incarnate.' After that incident in the pub Da came and told me what Paddy was after saying in answer to his 'How are you?' He was very much hurt by that.

The Grannie was the queen bee in Russell Street, sitting up in bed marking the neighbours' rent books. She was in the top room of the biggest tenement house, and the tenants of five or six houses had to bring the rent – and the talk – right up to her bed. They dared not leave her a week short, or out they went.

Sometimes the Grannie's son Paddy would be in the bed beside her. He slept with his mother right up to the age of thirty-five – until the day she died. There wasn't any harm in it, you understand – she just didn't want him taking up another room that she could let out for rent. That's all there was to it. It was a comical sight, though – a middle-aged baldy fellow lying there beside his mother. I couldn't understand it. My sisters and I wouldn't wash ourselves in front of our brothers, yet here were these two sleeping in the same bed (and using the po under it). They ate and slept in that same room for all those years.

And, I found out later, drank in it. You see, God help her, she had a terrible bad leg . . . suffered seas of sorrow with that leg. So at night she would have to have a good drink of whiskey. When she died we found hundreds – well, dozens – of empty whiskey bottles hidden away at the back of the bed. She used to pour it out of a china teapot, so that the tenants wouldn't know. She would send out for it on the sly when we weren't there.

She had a gang of old cronies who would gather round her bed to give her all the news of the Street. First there were her two old sisters, Maggie and Jack – they called her Jack because she drank pints like a man, and smoked a pipe. She used to sell coal off a donkey and cart – she'd inherited the coal business from her husband when he died. When the nights were cold, she used to trundle the old donkey up the stairs and into her room for the night. If the donkey wouldn't move she would lift him – she was a powerful strong woman. It would give my children quite a fright to look at the velvet lugs of the donkey peeping round the stairs.

Another of her cronies was a Miss McHugh, who used to make mortuary habits for the dead. In the evening she would take some of her work into the Grannie's room and start sewing. She couldn't afford the light to work by in her own room. She sewed her own habit, and slept in it every night until she died. Her main customer for these mortuary habits was a nearby convent. She made the nuns' brown habits with a great big cross down the front of them – and the nuns paid her half nothing.

When Miss McHugh died, one of the nuns that she used to sew for asked me to show them her habit. When they had finished passing it round and admiring it, one of them said, 'And wasn't it well for her that she had us to work for?'

'Sure, you didn't half pay her,' I said back to the nun. 'She went blind sewing your habits on the cheap.'

'Then how did she live?' asked the nun.

'My mother-in-law kept her,' I said, and it was true. Even a mean old one like the Grannie looked after her friends. She told me once, 'Don't talk to me about freedom. You can starve as easily under the Green Flag as the Union Jack. Freedom from want is the only freedom worth having.'

That's not the end of the list of people buzzing round the Grannie's bed. There were also Paddy's women. Now, Paddy had gone bald at twenty, and always wore his cap – night, noon or morning, in bed or out of it. He couldn't bear anyone to see his bald head. Yet he had no shortage of women after him – him or his mother's money, you wouldn't know which. There were two in particular who seemed to spend all their time in the room, each afraid that if she left Paddy alone the other might come round and get an advantage. Once I saw the two of them wrestling over who would make Paddy's tea.

One of them was a silly girl just up from the country, who worked for the Grannie cleaning the houses. She was an iron fool, that one. One day she came up to Paddy in the lane, and whipped out a razor. 'Have me, Paddy, or I will cut my throat!'

Paddy was not a quick-thinking man. As she started sawing at her throat, he just stood and stared. Then I came round the corner, and saw her with the blood running out of her, and ran off to the barracks for the police. They took her to the hospital, where she was stitched up.

You may wonder what Paddy was doing all this time, once I'd run off for the police. There's no need to wonder really – he went off to Jemmy Gill's pub to steady his nerves after the dreadful experience. All the time we were fussing around with the police and the ambulance he was in there. It must have been hours. The rest of the story I heard from his friend, Mikey, and you really wouldn't believe it.

Mikey was standing at the corner of Russell Street debating with himself whether to go for a pint or go to the Strand Cinema, when out from Jemmy Gill's came Paddy, looking around him.

'How yeh, Mikey?' he asked, pulling a Woodbine from his pocket and lighting up. 'Is the paper man not around yet?'

Mikey said that he hadn't noticed, but the paper man was rarely late. And, just as he said that, around the corner of Jemmy Gill's came his familiar cry over the clatter of the traffic.

'I wonder is there any news worth reading at all, apart from me losers in the race?' Paddy asked, as he turned to cross the street.

Right where they were standing there was a newspaper placard. Mikey pointed at it, saying, 'Take a look at that beside you – there seems to be news enough about that.'

Paddy looked sideways at the placard, which read, 'Dublin Girl's Throat Cut!' 'Be God, now,' said Paddy, 'some poor bitch in trouble – or maybe some fella did it. Well, I'll get the paper and we'll see what it's about!'

As he dodged through the traffic, Mikey made up his mind to go for a pint, and followed him across the busy road. On the opposite side, where Paddy was having a chit-chat about his racing losses with the paper man, there were two men Mikey recognized coming round the corner. One wore a long black leather coat and soft hat, the other a light raincoat, also topped with a soft hat.

They were well known to the Rustlers as plain-clothes policemen. One was called Fifty, from his police number, and the other was always known as Brack – a shortening of his surname. As Paddy turned around, about to head back over the road, Fifty and Brack stopped in front of him. Paper in hand, Paddy gaped at them. He never had any dealings with the police, good, bad or indifferent, and always steered clear of the large gangs that sometimes formed at the corner. But he knew enough about them, and their methods of law administration, to dislike the very sight of them in uniform or civvies.

'Excuse me, sir,' said Fifty of the quaking Paddy, who nodded, trying to wet his very dry mouth with his tongue, and gain the courage to look up at the policeman.

'You live here in Russell Street?' cut in Brack.

Again Paddy nodded.

'Well, we wonder, sir, would you care to come back to the station with us?'

Paddy regained enough of his composure to speak back. 'Oh, hold on, hold on,' he spluttered. 'If you want me to join an identification parade, I'm sorry – but I have to go home to look after me sick mother!'

There was always an identification parade going on then at the police station, and many a fellow, or two or three, was pounced on at the corner to fill up a parade. That was one of the reasons that Paddy avoided that corner like the plague.

Fifty shook his head. 'Nothing like that at all,' he said, putting a hand on Paddy's shoulder. 'Just come along with us like a good man, will you?' And the two policemen steered poor Paddy off towards Fitzgibbon Street police station.

Mikey and the paper man stared after him in amazement. It wasn't like Paddy to be in trouble with those boys. Mikey went into the pub for his pint, but he hadn't been in there five minutes when in rushed little Joe Byrne, Paddy's drinking mate. He was paler than usual as he pushed his way to the counter and spread out his *Evening Herald*.

'Did yez read this, any of yez?' he said, pointing with shaking fingers at the front page. 'A young Dublin girl was admitted to Jervis Street Hospital this afternoon with a throat wound. The girl, with an address in Russell Street, was said to be in a serious condition.' The name the paper gave was, of course, that of Paddy's girl.

Mikey told the boys what he'd seen outside the pub shortly before. Soon the whole pub was talking.

'Son of Jasez!' exclaimed Joe. 'Our Paddy wouldn't hurt a fly, would he, fellas?'

'I wouldn't be so sure,' chipped in one of the 'ould wans' who sat in the corner. 'Jasez only knows what she saw in him, for she was a fine bit of a country girl – years younger than that oul waster.'

'Poor Paddy's had it,' groaned Joe. 'I knew something would happen between him and that mot!'

'He's had it all right,' chuckled the 'ould wans'.

But they had reckoned without the Grannie. As soon as she heard her beloved Paddy was in jail, she was down there – and soon Paddy was absolved from all blame with the law, 'to their satisfaction'.

This is how Paddy told the story, for years after the hue and cry had died down and the girl was released from the hospital. 'They wouldn't tell me a thing when they got me inside. They questioned me over and over about me movements that day, and then, what seemed hours later, they brought in a stranger. I knew immediately that he was a higher-up policeman, from the look of him. He asked me did I know "one Millie Gray" – and it was then I realized what it was all about. Word had got down to me mother, and Bejasez she flew up to the barracks. When she came in, I knew the bloody sparks would fly. When she had finished with the police and me, well, we *all* wished we had just gone up to Mountjoy jail, locked ourselves in solitary confinement, and shagged away the bloody key!'

But the last word around the Street was, of course, with the 'ould wans'. The 'ould wans' were the old women of Russell Street, some of them the Grannie's great cronies, others her bitter enemies. They had their special place to sit in the pub – and the biggest of the 'big fellows' wouldn't dare shift any of them out of it. They wore heavy black dresses – you wouldn't know how old their clothes would be – and their hands were all stained a dirty yellow from the constant pinches of snuff that they took. A juicy bit of scandal like the story I've just told was too good to die out, and the 'ould wans' let it live on as long as their wagging tongues permitted.

Losing the girlfriend who tried to cut her throat didn't seem to bother my brother-in-law Paddy much – there was soon another one fussing about the room waiting on him and his mother. I suppose it was some compensation for when he was a young boy, and the Grannie made him wait on her hand and foot. She kept him away from school to look after her, so he never had any education at all. Stephen, on the other hand, was reared like a typical Irishman – he wouldn't wash a cup. The Irishman's proudest boast is that he can't boil an egg. Their mothers bring them up like that, and when they're grown up their wives have to put up with it.

I never went as far as the Grannie, but I wasn't having my sons grow up like that, as I've said before. I always believed that women should be free, and servants to no man. I never knew a man that could really afford to keep a woman as a housekeeper. If he had to pay her every hour on the hour he'd be broke. Wives are cheap housekeepers – automatic dishwashers.

So I made sure my sons helped cook and clean. It made them all good husbands – not that I was worried about that then: I just wanted someone to help me. If they came in and asked, 'Where's my dinner?' I'd come back as smartly, 'Where's the servant – do you see any?' With nine of us in the family, I never idled a minute as it was.

It wasn't just the cooking and the cleaning – it's a lot of work clothing that many on little money. I'd knit every sock and jersey they ever wore – for seven children, and for my husband, and for my brother John in the country. For the rest of the clothes, I'd go down to Cole's Lane and look for secondhand things – that takes time, too. The only thing I ever got on the hire purchase was the footwear. That was so they wouldn't have wet feet. But if you bought anything else that way, you'd soon be broke. They robbed you with the interest you had to pay.

I once made a patchwork quilt. There were red patches, blue patches, green patches, every kind of patches – all sewn by hand. But I could never sew beautifully – there were stitches an inch thick in this quilt – and in the end it was so awful that I was ashamed to show it. My son Rory's wife makes beautiful quilts by hand, and whenever I see them I remember that one I made. It was very warm, though, so we used to put it on the bed with a good quilt to cover it. But it always troubled me, and at last I got fed up with it and gave it to the ragman. He was delighted to get it for the weight of rags. When Stephen came home that night the first thing he said was, 'Where's me quilt?' He never stopped for years. 'Where's me lovely quilt?'

We were poor, but Dublin was a wonderful city then. Here's another song by Peadar. It's one I love; it's called Anna Liffey after the River Liffey, you know, that flows through our city.

Down by Anna Liffey, my love and I did stray.
Where in the good old slush and mud, the sea gulls sport and play.
We got the whiff of ray and chips, and Mary softly sighed,
Ah, John, come along, for a one and a one down by the Liffey side.

One and one – that was fish and chips, of course.

Any mother will tell you that the best days of her life are when her children are around her. For ever after, no matter what they do, they're still her little children. And it was that way for me.

If you had a young baby in those days, everyone was your friend. They'd all help, and offer advice if the baby was sick.

Mind you, they had some queer ideas of how to look after a child – it's a wonder they didn't all die of infections.

Dublin was full of old women, the ends of their noses all brown from the snuff. They all took snuff – you'd see them with their tins offering each other a sniff off the back of their hands. Horrible, it looked; yet it wasn't so dirty a habit as smoking. Very few of the woman smoked then – I only started when I was eighty, though I've given it up again now.

Anyway, these old women were always willing to come in and help look after the children. But sometimes I would think the children might be safer left alone. There was one old custom that frightened me stiff – the old women would take a baby from the mother and swing it round and round by one leg. I wonder they survived that. Another thing these old women would do, and the mothers couldn't stop them, was to stick their dirty old thumbs dipped in sugar into a poor baby's mouth. Along with the sugar, of course, he'd get a mouthful of snuff, any kind of dirt you can think of, and every sort of germ. You'd think it would poison the child, wouldn't you?

Still, I had some ways then myself that they wouldn't let you get away with now. The only time I went into the pub before the age of sixty was to get a drink for my son Sean, who was a baby at the time. He was a very delicate baby, and once, when we were out with him, Stephen took me into a pub into Dorset Street and ordered half of whiskey for me.

When the gentleman brought my half of whiskey over, I asked him to put it in a bottle, '. . . and it'll do the baby'.

'Certainly, madam,' he said, and did it without blinking.

I often used to give the children a teaspoon of whiskey to keep off the cold. That was one thing, though; the way the Grannie used to carry on with Brendan was another.

I told you how she was a secret drinker. Well, by the time he reached the age of six she had Brendan on that lark too. Years later, when Brendan was famous, one reporter asked me what had driven him to drink. Was it the rows he had with his father? 'That's all codology,' I said. 'It was his Grannie that led him astray.'

The Grannie adored Brendan, as I've said. He could do no wrong in her eyes. They used to go off to wakes and weddings, the pair of them, her an old woman and him just a little chissler – a fine pair of drunkards! She used to send him out for her beer – that's how he got to like it. She would send him for a pint in a jug – at that time you could take a jug to the pub and they'd fill it for you – but on the way back he'd drink half of it and then fill it up with water. She never even noticed – blinded with adoration, I suppose.

You'd think a six-year-old drunkard would be difficult to rear, but you'd be wrong. Brendan was the quietest child that was ever born or reared. None of my children were troublesome – they were all very good. Before Brendan would go out he would kneel down in the basement, join up his hands and look up to Heaven and say his prayers. I wanted my children to be religious, though now I'm not so sure about religion myself.

The other thing I wanted for them was to learn Irish. Well, some did and some didn't. It was quite an expense schooling children then – even with the Christian Brothers. I had to provide all their school books and copy books for their lessons. The copy books were the worst – one one week and one another. With the school books, when the older ones were finished with them you gave them to the younger ones. I believe you can't do that now. They have different lesson books every year. It makes a lot of money for the people that write them, I suppose, but what about the poor mothers?

I wanted them all to learn Irish, because it seemed right then, but I don't agree with teaching everything in the schools in Gaelic, as they do now. Brendan had a good phrase for it. 'The Education Minister is making us illiterate in two languages, English and Irish,' he said when they brought that in. It's the lessons that matter, not the language they're taught in – it only makes it harder for the poor to better themselves.

I told you about the great walks we used to have, me and a great load of children like a school outing. Some funny things used to happen on those walks – though at the time they'd drive my frantic. With seven of them to keep an eye on, it sometimes seemed I couldn't leave the house without losing either a child or the bus fare home. We went out one day to get blackberries at Whitehall, or maybe Santry, I forget which – anyway it was a long way out. We had one shilling for the fare home, and it got dropped in among the bushes. It was quite impossible to find with the thorns and the briars, so it was a three-mile walk home for the eight of us – one a baby in my arms.

I always thought it was a crime, children living in the slums and never seeing the sea. I used often to take mine down to the Bull Wall at the mouth of the Liffey. You have to watch your step round there, as the ground is full of holes the soldiers made during the First World War, and the grass by then had grown up and you wouldn't know where the holes were.

The whole family – Stephen and me and the seven children – had packed up after a great afternoon down at the Wall. Stephen and I walked ahead, with the children running around behind us in ones and twos. Suddenly I missed Brendan. It's hard to keep tabs on a lot of children when they don't want to go home and keep running off, but a mother will miss one if she has twenty with her, I think. I said to Stephen, 'Where's Brendan?' He shook his head.

Away back we went, and walked for what seemed miles. Even then we would have missed him, I think, but for his shouting. Thank God he was a bold boy, spoiled by his Grannie, for he was shouting fit to blow your ears off: 'Are yez blind or what – or is it that you want to get rid of me?' And he was only eight! That's how we found him, for he was stuck in one of those holes in the long grass, with only his head sticking out. God love him, his little round face and his curls sticking out of the hole – I couldn't be cross with him, I was so relieved.

He couldn't get out of the hole. As fast as he tried, the loose sand just poured in round him and all but smothered him. He was hanging on to the sides of the hole by his fingertips when Stephen rushed up and pulled him out. Much gratitude he got – only more 'Are yez blind?'

We nearly lost a writer there – and we nearly lost a singer

when Dominic fell in the canal. I don't know how he did it – he managed not only to fall in, but to get his head stuck in an old bucket that was lying on the bottom. It was his boots that saved him. They were good strong leather boots – as I said, I never bought rubbish for my children's feet – and they were a couple of sizes big, for him to grow into. This meant they acted as a sort of float, and a neighbour saw them and pulled him out feet first. He was a sorry sight when he was brought home – wet like a drowned cat and with the dirty canal water sloshing out of his boots.

All my children were fond of reading. I suppose it was in them. But they didn't get a lot of schooling once we had come to Crumlin from Russell Street, because they had to change from one school to another and it upset them terribly.

They were all clever children. I never made favourites of any of them – they were all the same to me. Although people think Brendan was a pet of mine, he wasn't. Da's mother petted him a terrible lot, as I've said, but I didn't. Brendan was very like his father in appearance, but I'd say he took after my brother, Peadar Kearney, though of course Da was intelligent too. He took after both sides of the family.

I never had any hopes of any of them being writers. And I have always been happy because, although they write, they have their trade if anything ever happens. They'll never be poor. It's a great thing to have a trade.

I think Brendan was writing when he was in the infants' school, because Sister Monica (who was fifty years in that school in North William Street – she loved boys and she loved Brendan) said, I remember, when I went down to her to complain of Brendan being naughty, 'Mrs Behan, are you aware you are rearing a genius?'

'Genius or not,' said I, 'he can be a bold lump when he likes.' I didn't care what he was as long as he was good.

She was very sad when I cut his curls off; he had lovely brown curls. When she died all Dublin turned out. She had reared hundreds of Dublin boys. She was a wonderful woman, and Brendan never forgot her.

Sister Monica showed me Brendan's books. He was first-class in everything – English, spelling, arithmetic. I went to his old school not long ago with the Lord Mayor. They took the old books out again and told the children what a great man he was. I don't suppose the children could bother their bums about him. Still, they gave a great cheer when the Lord Mayor said they could have a day off in his honour. Would you believe it – for our Brendan? Oh, he was a lovely child, but terrible nervous – he had an awful stammer. Later on in life it would come back if he got very nervous.

Da used to read for me – for I had poor eyesight – indeed he read for us all. Dickens, Thackeray, all the greats. He would read for hours with the children listening to him. It's something every mother and father should do, encourage reading: there's nothing better for a child's imagination.

On a summer evening in Russell Street the place was alive with children. There might be as many as fifty out on the Street, playing all day and most of the evening. All sorts of games they played – relivo, hopscotch and every-inch-a-punch. That was a game where one child would stand against the wall, another would form a long back, and the rest would jump on their backs. They loved these rowdy games – violent games – but they meant no harm by them, and the mothers knew their children were safe.

It was a different story on the housing estate we moved to later, the Crumlin estate. There, they said, the kids played tip and tag with hatchets. I don't know about that, but it's a fact that the mothers didn't look after them as well as we did in Russell Street. The children would come home and the mother would be in the pub. When my children came home, the coal cellar was the furthest away I ever was. We can see the fruits of that way of going on now: the noise the children make, the vandalism and the foul language they use. The smallest child in Crumlin now uses words that would make the old bowsies of Russell Street blush when they were sober – or even when they were drunk. And they can be so cruel to animals now. I saw two children killing a swan on the canal once – they didn't think anything of it. They just got up a stone and left the swan dead. This is what happens when the mothers forget their children.

My children were usually gentle with animals. They didn't even like to see the cats catch the rats. Brian was very upset once when our cat Snowy caught a pigeon. I remember seeing the cat holding the pigeon and the poor thing looking at the cat with its great unwinking eyes – and Brian hardly able to bear it but unable to take his eyes away as Snowy pulled the bird to bits. Ever since then, he says, he's rated cats as the Fascists of the animal world. We had to have a cat, though, or we'd have been eaten alive with the rats. We had the Mountjoy brewery near us, and a man told me it attracted all the rats for miles – all the malt, you see. This man said the rats swelled up with the porter until they were as big as dogs, and no cat could face them in his sober senses. Well, in that case our Snowy must have been a drinker on the sly.

All of us slum-dwellers thought that when De Valera came into power he would put boots on the footless. There was a song going round:

> God bless De Valera and Sean MacEntee
> For giving us brown bread and a half-ounce of tea.

So when he came in we all expected paradise on earth, but it turned out very different. He built those great housing estates, like something you'd see in Siberia. It was a terrible thing to move half the city out on to the sides of the mountains, without schools, buses or shops. Out in the slums we lived a rebellious, anarchic life that didn't suit the new Ireland at all.

I came to the conclusion there were things worth fighting for then. The Irish had been treated like dirt by the British occupation. They had all that was good in this world, the British had – fine houses, great wealth, good food, all the best land – and the Irish starved or slaved for the crumbs that fell from their tables. Any young fella with a drop of Irish blood in him had joined the Rebellion in 1916. That was the call, and men rallied to it. Yes, they considered it worthwhile.

But if you needed a job, and went to try at Brooks Thomas, the timber place, unless your dad had a good British Army or Navy discharge you were out. The same went for Arthur Guinness and Son, Player's cigarette factory, or any of the big shops in the city of Dublin. And should you go around some of the small building sites then, if the foreman on the job liked the look of you he told you to get your parish priest's reference, plus the local police sergeant's for good measure, before he could consider employing you.

Although we had our own Irish Free State government we still had the British at the helm as far as the working classes were concerned. The labour exchanges were besieged daily. Long queues of unemployed men, four deep, spun from Gardiner Street labour exchange to the opposite side of Abbey Street, facing across to the Abbey Theatre. Families tried to get extra relief from the St Vincent De Paul Society. These good people visited each and every family in a street, doling out half a crown's worth of goods by voucher or maybe the half crown itself. The kids of Russell Street would catcall and jeer as the St Vincent's men paid each their weekly visit. Peculiar, you know, when you come to think of it – Irish children making fun of each other's poverty. Just like the Irish – they love to wallow in someone else's misery.

I might be wrong, but I am convinced that that particular brand of fun was instilled by the British. I used to read their comic cuts regularly when I was much younger, and I remember two characters in a pink comic called *Chips*. Weary Willie and Tired Tim were their names, and they were two down-and-out tramps. Each week they tried to do an odd job, and usually ended up banjaxing it. It would seem to me that the British upper class poked that type of fun at the poorer class, who were portrayed as layabouts, tramps and workshies who could not and would not do an hour's honest work when offered it. Look at the attitude the workers here adopted, when a bit of work occurred. Tradesmen and labourers, never the twain shall meet, was the way they set about a building job. No painter, bricklayer, plumber or carpenter entertained a labourer. They sat in separate groups at the tea break – the labourers on one side, the tradesmen on the other.

In the thirties they opened soup kitchens. Of course, people didn't like to be seen going down to them, so they'd send their children over. The children would rush home with a great bowl of the purest water: 'Nanny water,' Stephen called it. I remember dividing a loaf up among seven. Worse, I remember when we were reduced to eating a pincushion. I used to make them out of a bit of rag, which I'd fill with oatmeal. One day when we were strapped with hunger and I could stand it no more I took the pincushion and (remembering to take all the pins out first) ripped it apart and boiled up all the oatmeal inside. Horrible, it was: all dust and fluff, easily the worst meal any of us have ever had. But it filled our bellies for a while and we were glad enough at that. We had to manage whatever way we could.

That's how things were when the building trade was slack. Then the only way we could get money was to go off to the pawn shop. I always thought the pawnbrokers were the friend of the working-class person, strange though that might sound today. Who else would loan us money? Stephen used to pawn his paper cutter every week for years. In the end they were so used to seeing it go in and out they didn't bother to open the little box to look at it. So one day he put a stone in the box, and walked in and plonked it on the counter. The poor pawn office man just called out, 'Two pounds and the name is Behan.' I suppose it's still there to this day, waiting to be reclaimed. Stephen said it was the dearest stone outside a diamond mine.

When all the pledges were in pawn there was one last resort.

I would have to steal half a crown from the Grannie – that's the only guilty secret of my life. But still she had plenty of money, taken from those that had nothing, and all I wanted it for was the children. I don't believe that would be a sin at all. It's not as if we had anything else. She would be in bed, of course, and she would send me over to the dresser to get something for her; and there would be the money on top. She would never spot me slipping half a crown into my apron. It might be that she would have given me the money if I'd asked, but she was a strange old woman and you could never tell.

So when the trade was down it was a matter of pawning and smuggling out half crowns. But if there *was* any work in the trade, Stephen was sure to get it – he was the best painter in Dublin. So for much of the time we had a steady income – though I never knew how much. Stephen kept a lot back to spend down the pub. But he'd give me enough to feed us all well, when he had it.

That was a ceremony in every house, when the man handed over the wages each week. My brother Peadar had a God Almighty row with his wife once. When he came in, he didn't *hand* her the wages, but put them on the mantlepiece. She wouldn't have that. Quite right too – it was degrading, as if she were some kind of lodging-house keeper, not the woman of the house. So she wouldn't take the money off the mantlepiece, but waited for him to put it into her hand. They both sat there for a time, staring at this money and at each other, and in the end, without a word, my brother took the money off the mantlepiece himself and took it down to the pub. That was it for the rest of the week for them. Still, they made it up later.

Another woman I knew had a disaster once with her husband's wage packet. We always used to sit at the table to peel the potatoes for dinner, putting the skins in the middle of the table to throw away. Well, one day her husband came in while she was doing the potatoes, and put the money down on the table, which was their habit. Then they made a cup of tea and talked for a while, and then she gathered up the potato

Kathleen Behan, photographed by Brian Behan

The painting of Kathleen Behan as a young woman, by Sarah Purser, only recently identified

Opposite above: Kathleen with Sean and Rory, 1921
Below: 70 Kildare Road, 'the Christlike Kremlin', as accurately reconstructed by RTE for its dramatization of 'Teems of Times', the Behan family story by Dominic Behan. Note the picture of Christ hanging between Connolly and Lenin

Top: Kathleen and Stephen, *c.* 1960. The children have gone out for a jar
Above: 'Stephen Behan, This is Your Life': the Dublin recording. The photo shows
(sitting, left to right) Kathleen, Stephen and Jimmy Kearney, and (standing)
Rory, Joseph Paton (Carmel's husband), Carmel, Brian, Dominic, Con Kearney
(Peadar Kearney's son), his wife, Pearse Kearney and Eamonn Andrews

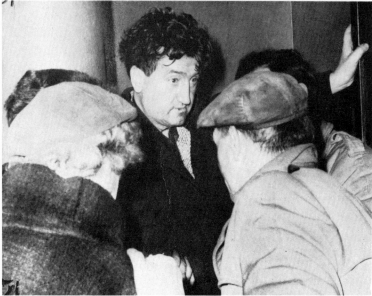

Top: Brendan in a London pub with Joan Littlewood, at the time of *The Hostage*, planning 'to divert the public with a song and a dance' (Brendan)
Above: Last days of a golden boy: Brendan, photographed in Phil O'Reilly's bar, Dublin, a few days before he was taken to hospital for the last time. Kathleen is in the left foreground

At the graveside:
Kathleen and
Stephen, Beatrice and
Dominic at Brendan's
funeral

Opposite
Kathleen at the
unveiling of the
plaque
commemorating
Brendan's life at 70
Kildare Road,
Crumlin

Kathleen outside 14 Russell Street

skins and threw them into the fire. And, yes, you've guessed it, threw in his wages along with them! She never lived that one down.

Anyway, assuming that there were any wages, and they hadn't got drunk up or burned up, what did we spend them on? When the children were young I used to buy a whole sack of potatoes for a single meal. A whole batch of bread – maybe four loaves at a time. I'd buy a couple of pounds of black and white pudding – more black than white – and streels of sausages. When you've seven growing children you can't go in for this fancy cooking; you have to buy what will fill them up and what they like. A great favourite was beef tea. I'd take a whole pound of stewing beef, put it in water and gently simmer it for an hour or two. It was lovely – do your heart good.

I wonder how the poor and the unemployed do nowadays. Not so well as we did, I would guess. The markets were better in those days. You could buy stuff cheap and be sure it was fresh – now it's all supermarkets. The poor housewife has no choice, has she? I used to take the children down to Moore Street on a Saturday morning, and it was a great way to shop, listening to all the old dealers.

'Three a penny the oranges!'

'A penny a pound them fresh onions!'

'Here, missus, give him some of these and he won't let you alone for a week!'

Weren't they as common as ditchwater? I used to buy a bit of rabbit, a few potatoes, a few sausages, and make what we called a coddle – a lovely hot dish, and Stephen said it put hair on his chest. They talk about the bad old days, and they were bad enough, God knows, but where can you get that sort of thing now?

So we weren't among the very poorest of the poor. In fact, if Stephen had been a bit more careful, we'd have been on the pig's back. My sister used to say that he drank a couple of houses in the pubs. You could have bought one from the

dregs. Maggie, who'd worked every hour God sent and some
he didn't to build up her business, never drank herself and
neither did her husband. She was right, of course, but I don't
think she understood Stephen's need for a drink and company
after working hard all day. Not that I liked Stephen coming
home drunk. Some time after he returned from prison I went
in and asked his mother if she knew any way to stop it.

'I will give you the cure for him,' said the Grannie. 'Yez just
wait behind the door, and the next time he comes in so drunk
he doesn't know his own religion, then just you up and down
him with the heaviest pot you can lay your hands on.'

'Oh, no,' says I, 'I might kill him!'

'Divil a bit of it – he has a head on him like the Rock of
Cashel.'

Well, I thought, his own mother ought to know what she
was talking about. So, the very next time, I did it – I knocked
him on the head with an iron cooking-pot; and down he went,
clean out. But did it bother him? Not a bit of it – he just lay
there and slept like a baby till morning. The following day he
couldn't remember a thing. Many's the good laugh we had
about it in later years; but it scared me stiff at the time – *and* it
didn't stop him going out.

It was the company that he went out for. In the Dublin pubs
you have the meeting of the waters – they're where all the
classes mix. I don't think it's the same in other countries. And,
to be honest, he didn't want to be bothered with the children
all the time. He would like to come in when they'd all gone to
bed. They, in turn, didn't care at all for him staggering about
and talking nonsense. I was always telling them, 'Get to bed
quick, before your father comes in', and they'd go to bed like a
shot. When he looked in at them they would pretend to be
asleep.

So for much of the time I was all alone of an evening. As
Brendan grew older, he let me know that he didn't like it. He
would stay in with me if Stephen was out. I think that was what
led to their later quarrels: Brendan thought Stephen had not
treated me as the woman of the house should be. Yet all of

them – the Grannie, Stephen and Brendan – had the same contempt for the day-to-day troubles that had the likes of me worried. 'Everything will be all right,' were Stephen's words for any difficulty.

Brendan was right, though, to say that Stephen didn't do enough in the house. He might have been the best painter in Dublin, but you should have seen our walls! Our hall door was hanging off for want of a coat of paint. When we moved to Crumlin, later, we had a bit of garden, and I asked Stephen if he'd mind planting a few cabbages. 'Why?' he asked. 'Are all the greengrocers closed?' He would leave a week's dishes lying in the sink as long as there was a clean cup for his tea. No matter what you said to him, it was 'Come day, go day, God send Sunday . . . It'll all be there when I'm dead, that's all – no use worrying about it.'

I don't want to give the impression that Russell Street was the worst slum in Dublin. In fact, it was more on the fringes of Slumdom (though, Heaven knows, nobody today would put up with the conditions there). For all the overflowing lavatories and the fights between the drunken old bowsies, I was living like a queen compared to the people in the Diamond. That's the area around Sean MacDermott Street, where I'd lived as a child. In Russell Street I lived daily with the war between the IRA and the government – in the Diamond it was nothing so civilized, it was gang warfare.

The main gang was the Animal Gang – a set of bandits, really, who used to utter terrible animal cries as they grabbed their victims, to rob them or rape them or sometimes just to give them a fright. They started up in the early twenties, and they made the streets they controlled no-go areas for the police. I believe there were some six hundred of them at one time.

Though the official government could, it seemed, do nothing to stop them, the unofficial government – the IRA – used to pursue them. The Republicans finally decided to show them a lesson when some IRA girls selling Easter lilies were beaten up and robbed. That night, a group of men simply drove down into the Diamond and knee-capped the gang leaders. This was quite effective, for a while – at least nobody with any IRA connections got bothered. And it showed the people that the IRA could get things done, which was more than the Free Staters could do.

Still, they didn't wipe the gang out – in fact I heard that the city centre has once again been declared bandit territory. Brendan had a brush with them some years later. Apart from robbing people, the gang made money out of running gambling dens. These were seen as fair game by the Republicans when they needed money. Brendan went into one with a gun and swept up the money, solemnly declaring, 'I am taking this money for the cause of the Republic.'

He was almost out when one of the gamblers, who had seen him around the pubs, stood up. 'You're an effing liar, Behan! The only cause you're thinking of is the cause of Arthur Guinness!'

I always dreaded the winter, which was a slack time in the building trade. Sometimes it would be hard to buy coal to cook on, let alone any food. Yet we always managed to have a feast at Christmas. The Grannie would give us a goose or a fine turkey, as I mentioned earlier, and the Bourkes (my sister and her husband) would send down a ham. It might together be more than we'd eaten all month, but we gobbled it all up over the holiday. And I would think that maybe those three terrible Behans – Stephen, Brendan and the Grannie – were right after all, and we shouldn't burden ourselves with worry: everything would be all right in the end.

I'm sorry to say, though, that those three all quarrelled later. Brendan and Stephen did not get on when Brendan was grown; I've told you why I think that was. Stephen and his mother also fell out, and were not speaking when she died. It was partly over Brendan – though Stephen treated the children all alike, he was the first-born son, and the Grannie did spoil him and take him away from his father. There was also a row about a club she was running. You paid in so much a week, and when your week came round you took all the money that had been collected that week. When it was Stephen's week for the share-out she said, 'Sure, you *owe* me twice as much as that.' It was quite true: she was always loaning us money when we were short. But Stephen just walked out of the room and never spoke to her again.

Six months later she was dying. I went to Stephen and told him, but all he said was, 'Dish me up my dinner.'

Then I said, 'But if you don't go up now, you won't see your mother – she's passing out.'

But he just said again, 'Dish me up my dinner.'

This quarrel of theirs broke me up. I always tried to bring people together, not build up walls between them. But they were all so stubborn, that family of mine, that it was quite beyond me.

As I said, we began the early part of the thirties in Russell Street. It was a time of big changes in our lives. In the first place the Long Fellow – Da called him a long streak of misery – De Valera was elected prime minister. We had supported Fianna Fail through thick and thin, and Da had even been jailed by the Free Staters, if you recall, so you can be sure we lit bonfires in the middle of Russell Street to celebrate Dev's great victory. The people were all for him. He told us that the resources of Ireland were so great that to develop them he would have to bring the emigrants back from America. God bless the mark, he did no such thing. Only sent all the more.

The Grannie just laughed at us. 'God give you sense, girl,' said she. 'What does it matter to the likes of us who is in power? . . . There was a man once, riding along the road in County Clare, when a poor man breaking stones by the roadside for council raised his head and asked the man who had won the election. The man on the horse looked down and replied, "It's all the same to you, poor man, because whoever did win you will still be breaking those stones tomorrow morning."'

Well, we were the same. We had in charge of us a pure lunatic. He wanted an Ireland Gaelic, free and holy, but he made us sup sorrow with a long spoon. First of all he started the economic war. We wouldn't send any cows to the English market. One good thing – at least this gave us free beef for the first time in our lives. We sang a song the year he was elected: 'And We'll Crown De Valera King of Ireland'. We were always looking for kings, weren't we? A strange tack for Republicans.

The Grannie was right – she was a shrewd one and no mistake. But then at the age of eighty-four she died, and our life at Russell Street died with her.

5

The Move to Crumlin

*'If there is a Heaven it must be for
working women'*

After the Grannie's death in 1935 the Behans learnt
that the tenements in which they had been living had
been condemned. They moved to a small house at
Crumlin, way outside Dublin, leaving behind the
squalor and overcrowding of Russell Street but also its
strong community spirit

The Grannie always said that, when she died, she wanted fine fat-arsed black horses to take her to the cemetery, not skinny old knackers. 'Let them have great black plumes leaping and rearing out of their heads,' she used to say – and we saw to it that she got them. Funerals then were grand occasions. The body would be laid to rest at the chapel for a couple of days, then the procession would take the body twice round the area, passing the house twice, and ending up at the graveyard. Everyone saved for their funeral then – not like today – so it was a great party for all the neighbourhood. The processions were all the same. First you would get the best carriages, then the poorer ones, then people on bicycles, and last of all people walking – them that couldn't afford either a carriage or a bicycle. They would stop at every pub on the way, and by the time they reached the graveyard they were fairly staggering. And it was so for the Grannie. She might have taken money all her life from the people in her houses, but in death she all but gave it back again. Still, I couldn't help thinking that she'd have to answer to God for taking the money off poor people that hadn't any.

After she was dead I found out all her secrets. First there were the whiskey bottles behind the bed. I told you that she used to pour the whiskey out of a china teapot so that the neighbours wouldn't know. Then, while sorting her things, I found a letter from the Corporation. It surprised me because it said that most of the houses were condemned – and that meant she wasn't entitled to charge a penny rent. She was kind to us, but for the tenants, she'd take the eyes out of their heads and come back for the lashes.

Still, now her property wasn't our business anyway. Having quarrelled so badly with Stephen, she left all the money to Paddy – and he wouldn't let us have a penny of it. He was so mean – even if he were a ghost he wouldn't give you a fright. Stephen was very bitter – but he had refused to see her before she died, even though she had asked for him.

The Grannie left £3000, which was an awful lot of money in 1935. Would you believe that Paddy drank the lot in nine months – him and his two old aunts, Maggie and Jack? It killed him, too. No wonder Stephen felt he was hard done by.

Almost immediately we moved out. I'd been on at Stephen for years to move away from Russell Street, but he had always hated the idea. We could have taken a purchase house: you could buy them for just shillings a week, and they were yours after twenty years. A friend of mine took one about the same time as we moved – a lovely house just off the Clonliffe Road, far nicer than the one we went to. But Stephen wouldn't have it, because a purchase house would be fifteen shillings a week – ten went towards buying it. So for us it was off to Kildare Road, Crumlin. It seemed like a thousand miles from the city and the people we loved, where everyone was ready to help everyone else, and where there were plenty of pubs nearby so that we could always meet our friends and have a bit of a sing-song and a laugh. When he first heard about Crumlin Da was horrified. 'My God, Kathleen,' says he, 'sure they eat their dead out there.'

We had gone down, year in, year out, to the Housing Department of the Corporation. We should have had a house years before that, with nine of us living in two rooms. But there were people even worse off than us, and the ones who got houses first were the ones with TB. Well, one day I went down, and Mr Marks in the office told me, 'Good news, Mrs Behan. You have a house if you want it. Do you?'

'Would a duck swim?' say I, grabbing the key.

90

I dragged Da out to look at the house on the Sunday before we moved. We had the trams that time – they ran out to Dolphin's Barn and then you walked. It was miles away. Sacred heart of God, I nearly died. I thought we were going to Siberia. Crumlin, you know, is right out of the city, on the slopes of the Dublin Mountains. It would put your heart crossways, just looking at miles and miles of new roads. No lights. It was like the Wild West. Da cursed and swore about leaving his dirty old pub and being miles away from his work, but I didn't care. *He* didn't have to put up with one lavatory used by seven families, because he spent most of his time in that pub, so Russell Street suited him. The wind would take the skin off your bones that day. What with Da stumbling here and there he almost fell down a ditch. It was no joke, I can tell you.

At last we reached Kildare Road. The little house was lovely – it's still there today. It has a plaque over the door now, put up by locals to honour Brendan. (It was made by a famous Dublin sculptor, John Behan – no relation, but as good to me as any son.) Anyway, I wouldn't call the queen my aunt just to be there in that house. Is there anything better than the smell of fresh paint? I was delighted. Tiny it was, with a little front parlour and two little bedrooms, but that was still better than all of us stuck in two rooms.

Even then Da didn't want to take it, making up all sorts of excuses. 'There's no buses,' says he. 'No trams, no schools, no pubs, no nothing. Only miles of these houses stretching away into nowhere.' Well, I went for him. I told him move we would – Hell or high water. And we did.

I knew that previous to this Da had refused another offer of a house in Emmet Road. I told Rory and he said, 'Don't ask *him* to sign for anything, because he will stay in Russell Street for ever and it's getting worse.' Well, it was then that the Grannie died. A Mr Best acted as her agent and tried to look for the rent, but no one would pay him, and naturally the houses fell into rack and ruin. Rory said, 'Don't tell Da. *You* sign for the key.' I hired Mrs Farrell the coalman's cart – she sold coal either by the stone for fourpence or by the bag for two shillings and sixpence. She was another one that brought the oul ass up into her room to keep him warm.

Well, we threw our bits and pieces up on the cart and set off. We were just going by Jemmy Gill's pub when Da ran out, shouting, 'You're not going to Crumlin now, are yez?' We just kept on going all the way, and went up a place called the Dark Lanes in Crumlin. It was dark – no street lamps, as I've said – but Rory found some candles. We had to peer into gardens over mountains of clay until we found number seventy.

Crumlin was a desperate place when first we went there: no schools, no shops, nothing, except (as Brendan said) plenty of desolation. But I was glad enough in a way to go there; a house to yourself is better than rooms. It's good to have a clean home even if it's in the middle of nowhere.

There was a spirit in Russell Street that you could hardly imagine in Crumlin – that place knocked the spirit *out* of people. When the working man moved out there, it added hours to the day – travelling into the city – and it meant having to find the money for the bus fares on top of all the rest. So it isn't any real wonder that they began to lose their sense of freedom, the old devil-may-care rebel attitude. I was always for the working man, and it made me half sick to see these people broken down in despair. Not all at like those old bowsies I'd got used to.

Maybe Stephen was right not to want to pay out for a purchase house, for soon after we moved there began our hardest time of all: the great building strike of 1936. It was nine months long. Some of the bosses settled up, but Stephen, as leader of the union, couldn't go back to work until it was all over. It had been bad enough when he first came out of prison, but at least then there were fewer children, and the Grannie often helped out. Here on our own in Crumlin we nearly died. I begged and implored him to go to work, to let us eat at least.

His principles, he said, wouldn't allow it. I needn't tell you what I nearly said, but what I did say was, 'You can't eat principles, can you, Stephen?'

Still, at last they settled it and it was back to the old way of life. Crumlin didn't break my rebel spirit – in fact it stirred it up. God forgive me, I was a great supporter of Stalin. I reckoned that if the big pots were against him, he couldn't be all that bad. I thought he was the workers' friend. (Of course, everyone knows different now, but that's how it seemed then.)

So, just to stir the neighbours up as well, I used to play them the Russian National Anthem. Whenever any bit of it came on the radio, I'd turn it right up and open all the windows and just let them have it. After all, the people in Russell Street used to call me a 'bloody Communist', so you can imagine the Crumlin lot and what they said.

Anyway, in Crumlin I just wanted to shake them up a bit, because they weren't like that – they hadn't an ounce of spirit in them.

I liked the house in Crumlin, but I'm afraid Brendan hated it. A bit like Da, he said the people there were so savage they ate their children. I didn't find that: quite the opposite. I saw people driven mad trying to manage as best they could.

Brendan was about fourteen when he went there, and he said he missed the warmth of Russell Street. He thought the empty drab streets of the housing estate were cold comfort after the Street. He missed all the hallways. You know, children learned more about the facts of life in a hallway like that than they ever would out on the foot of the Dublin Mountains. That's why Crumlin was so cold – it was on the slopes of the hills. There again, Brendan missed all his friends from the Street. He would go over time and again, but it was no use – the Street was finished. The old houses, dirty and all as they were, he loved every brick in them. Cities change, I told him – like people, they have to renew themselves. But he never really got over the move. In his heart he was always a North Sider. The houses in Russell Street were fine big ones.

Every hall door had a great lion's head or sometimes a tiger's, out of which swung a great big knocker. Many and many's the time Brendan and the lads banged Hell out of that oul door. But you see, there was more in a great big street of Georgian houses for children to do.

During the Second World War I fought a battle with the Crumlin butchers. Although Ireland was not at war, we had food restrictions similar to those in Britain, and there were price controls on meat so that the poor could afford it even though it was short. But did the butchers take any notice? There were bits of meat that you could buy for a shilling a pound before, and people depended on those scraps for a dinner. Now the butchers were charging two shillings a pound.

One day the worst case of all came up. I was buying the Sunday joint, in a shop full of women on the same errand, and the butcher was charging everyone about ten shillings too much. When I reached the head of the queue I said, 'That's not the price of that!'

'It's my price,' the butcher said.

'But it's not the government price,' said I. 'I will let you see!' And I went straight down to the police barracks, and told them.

But none of the women in the shop would come to back me up. 'Who'd mind that bloody old Communist?' was all that they'd say. They were no help at all, yet I was only doing it for them.

So I had to take that butcher to court all by myself. I reported two more as well, including the one that used to sign the guarantee for the children's bicycles and so on.

He said to me afterwards, 'I never thought you would do that on the likes of me.'

So I asked him, 'Do your children eat meat?'

'Of course they do, Mrs Behan.'

'Well,' I said, 'the children in Crumlin don't, but as far as

I'm concerned I will see that they do, as far as I can. And I'm not one bit sorry that I summonsed you.'

When the cases came up in court, the judge looked down and saw that I was the witness for all three. 'You're a great woman, Mrs Behan,' he said.

But even then the Crumlin women wouldn't come along and help. They still just said, 'Who'd mind that bloody old Fenian?' You can't do a thing with some people.

One thing above all made the thirties and forties sad for me, and perhaps you'll say I have no real right to be sad about it. My children were growing up, and one by one in those years they left me – and most of them left Ireland too. The first hint of it came in the mid-thirties, when Brendan was fourteen. A letter came for him while he was out somewhere, and I just had a feeling about it. I was getting ready to go into the city with Brian to do the usual Saturday shopping. So I picked up that letter and put it into my pocket. I didn't want Brendan to come home while I was out, and then conceal whatever was in it from me when I got back.

Those shopping trips made Saturday a favourite day for Brian and me: riding on the tram back to the bustle of Moore Street, followed by tea and cakes at Bewley's coffee house. A little feast. (It's still there, and as good as ever.) But on this day I couldn't take my mind off that letter, so I opened it on the way home. Maybe that's something a mother should never do, but I did it, and when I read the letter I burst into tears. It was about Brendan going to Spain, to fight in the Civil War. It instructed him to meet a gentleman that was to take him there. I tore that letter up.

Brendan didn't find out until some years later, but when he did he never forgave me. Some of the family say I did the wrong thing to this day. He was already a man, they say; it should have been his decision, and he might have come back from the war a different Brendan. Yes, I say, but he might have come back no Brendan at all. You know the old song that my brother wrote:

> It was on the road to sweet Athy, horroo, horroo;
> It was on the road to sweet Athy, horroo;
> It was on the road to sweet Athy,
> With a stick in your hand and a tear in your eye;
> Why did you skedaddle from me and the child?
> Johnnie, I hardly knew you.
>
> Where are the legs with which you run, horroo, horroo?
> Where are the legs with which you run, horroo?
> Where are the legs with which you run,
> When first the Jerry pointed a gun?
> I'm thinking your dancing days are done.
> Johnnie, I hardly knew you.

Peadar wrote that about the First World War, but it sums up any woman's feelings about her menfolk going off to any foreign war. Besides, even if Brendan had come back in one piece, a reformed character, would he have then become the great writer we all remember? All these years later I still think I did right.

Not that Brendan wasn't right in wanting to fight for the Republicans in Spain. All the priests in Dublin were for Franco, as I've told you before. They told the Irish people to be for him too, when of course they should have been for the Republicans. Brian told me of an incident at school, when the Christian Brothers were condemning the Reds in Spain. Up he spoke and said, 'But aren't they the lawfully constituted government, and doesn't the catechism tell us to honour those whom God has placed over us? Isn't Franco just a rebel?' Of course he got a slap in the face for his pains.

As I told you, Crumlin was a cold place and it got colder still with hunger. By the latter part of the thirties, it was hard to manage. More and more people were out of work, and everything in Crumlin was dear. In Russell Street you could have lived for years on tick. If you went to the Fat Man's shop he would put it in the book till next week. Then again, in Russell Street you were near all the markets and secondhand shops. In Crumlin we had none of that. Only long lines of thousands of houses, each and every one the same. No buses either, and if you walked down to Dolphin's Barn there was a long, expensive tram ride into the city.

I had to make ends meet. Many's the time I thought I would run away and do something else, but there was nowhere to run to. You had to stand your ground, though many a poor working woman ended up in a mental home. If there is a Heaven, it must be for working women. It won't be for nuns – they have no strain compared with a woman running a family. It was Hell on earth telling all my sons, 'You can't eat this or that, because it has to be left for your father.' But what else could we do? Occasionally I would cook an egg for Da's breakfast and I would watch him eat it. Sometimes he would lop the top off the egg and give it to one of the lads. Then again they could dip their bread in it. Looking back, in Russell Street we had years of plenty.

We were so poor that the lads would go on to the Corporation rubbish dump and salvage apples or anything. One day they brought home a great box of chocolates. Then they would start digging for old coal and cinders in the hot ash. One lad was buried alive, because they built great tunnels down into the dump to get at the cinders, and one of them collapsed on him. You couldn't believe how poor we were. I tried to sell two old vases to a friend for a shilling, just to buy a bit of tea and that. Mind you, one advantage we had then over people now was that you could buy everything in ounces: tea, sugar, anything. There were little amounts for poor people. Even cigarettes you could buy one for a penny. Of course, it was dearer buying things that way, but if that was all you had, that was what you had to do. I always tried to send the children to bed full no matter how I did myself. But it was an awful time trying to manage on half nothing.

Yes, poverty laid a heavy hand on my family in the late thirties. It shook our house and started to beat the lard out of us. A family can only stand the grinding so long, and then something has to give. Da never missed an hour's work in his life when he could get it. But it wasn't that plentiful, and then the strike lasting nine months put us back years. The working man never recovers from a long strike. Everything you have saved, every penny you have spared, has to go.

And then in our greatest hour we had no Russell Street to fall back on. We had new houses, but rent to pay. In the old slums we wouldn't pay God Almighty. The neighbours in the Street were kindness itself, too. But then we had the open hall doors, and everyone lived within a stone's throw of each other, some of them just next door in the tenement. Dominic has written a history of the Street, called *Teems of Times*, and it has been on the television. He showed that they would put their eyes out on sticks for you in Russell Street – they would do *anything* for a body. The neighbours in Crumlin were good people but they were isolated and scattered, and it takes years to get to know anyone in an estate, if you ever do. In our little boxes in Crumlin all we knew in the first years was poverty, hunger and rent.

Still, another great writer apart from Brendan came out of Crumlin, or rather moved there like us. *He* moved in an old orange box – he was paralysed. His mother never gave up her home, and even though he was one of thirteen children she spent hours with him, teaching him little movements. Eventually he typed out a book with his toes (he hadn't the use of his arms) and, God bless the mark, it became a bestseller. His name was Christy Brown, and his book was called *Down All the Days*. Brendan said he was a great writer, with or without feet. He's dead now too – swallowed a lump of fatty bacon and away he went. Wasn't it marvellous, just when he was on the pig's back, moved into a new house in the country with a new wife, and then he chokes to death on a bit of meat?

Of course my lads were really young men now, and getting harder to feed – eating like horses when they could get it. As

Da was growing older I told the biggest lads, 'Aren't you ashamed to live and eat idle bread, while a poor grey-haired man goes out to work to feed you?' I know it sounds hard, but the times *were* hard. One of the lads did apply for assistance, and we had the means test man around. We had to hide everything of any value – not that it was much. And, worst of all, we had to make the *beal bocht* – that's Irish for the poor mouth. Poverty makes beggars out of people, and they never forget. People who experienced unemployment and real poverty in the thirties will never feel full, no matter how much they eat. It sits in the mind forever. Still, the assistance people gave us nothing. Instead they told us that if a son lived with his parents he must be kept by them, be he five or fifty.

As it happened, we were soon to have less mouths to feed, but not quite in the way that we would have wished.

6
The Family Breaks Up

'There's no love like a mother's, but children don't know that'

Political activity had always been a part of the Behans' daily lives, and as the children grew up and left home for some of them – Brendan in particular – it became the central focus of their lives. Inevitably it is stories about Brendan's escapades in and out of prison that dominate Kathleen's recollection of the forties, though Brian and Dominic, too, were deeply involved in trade unions

At the age of twelve Brian went into an approved school. He mitched from school, and in the end off he went. Brendan wrote to him from Liverpool when he was in Borstal, which I'll tell you about in a moment. I took the letter out to Brian. 'Keep your heart up,' Brendan said. 'The darkest hour is before the dawn.'

The school was in the village of Artane, and held hundreds of boys. Brian was sentenced to four years in detention there. It broke my heart to stand with Da in front of the children's judge, old McCarthy, and hear Brian committed, but what else could we do? Children would break the heart in a body, wouldn't they? There's no love like a mother's but children don't know that.

The regime was tough. The Christian Brothers who ran it said they were preparing them for the hard world that lay ahead, but after Artane you could survive Belsen. They had to be up at six, winter or summer, strip off, cold wash and then an hour's prayers. Brian had to work for eight hours a day, first in a laundry and then in a bakehouse. Then they had school from five to seven. Still, each and every child had a trade when he came out, and that was the school's aim – it was an industrial school, and the Brothers never liked it being called an approved school.

The Brothers were true vegetarians – for the boys, that is. The lads never saw a bit of meat from one end of the year to another. Every Brother was named after a saint, and each of them had a feast day to celebrate the saint's anniversary, so, as you can imagine, with two hundred Brothers there were lots of feasts. Da got Brian released early – he only did two years and eight months.

Some of the lads were foundlings left outside convents when they were babies by poor girls too frightened, or too poor, to keep them. These lads never knew anything else but the home, from the day they were born until they were sixteen years of age. You could see them sitting silently on the benches along with the other lads, waiting for ever, with no one to come.

They had a different language in there. Brian used to come out on visits once every six weeks and we couldn't understand him. The Christian Brothers were so afraid of impurity that they used to call things by completely different names. A lad's bottom became his chest, and his willy became his finger.

The Brothers were very hard, but they had to be – they were trying to rear all these lads and instil respect and fear of the Lord into them. And they tried to teach them a trade: Brian became a baker. They had a wonderful band and a wonderful football team. Brian was a very good Gaelic footballer – he was football-mad. Eventually he played for the Army. I went to see him in our national stadium, Croke Park.

So by the end of the thirties Rory was in the army, and Brendan and Brian were gone, hardly ever to return home again. Brian was at Artane and Brendan was to begin a sentence in Borstal. Little did I think that Brendan would spend almost half his adult life in one prison or another.

We just couldn't keep our Brendan out of the fray for long. One way or another, he had to be in it. He went over to Liverpool in the late thirties and, as everyone knows, was sentenced to three years' Borstal for possessing explosives. The judge couldn't believe that he was only sixteen. It was lucky that was all that he was – if he had been any older he would have got fourteen years. The governor said he was released early after giving a promise not to do anything until the Hitler war was over. Da denied that and said publicly, 'It is not a custom for our lads to say things like that, and Brendan's promise was contrary to our IRA code.'

I said to Da, 'You need not have said that to the papers about Brendan, but you always said more than your prayers.'

Still, Brendan was safe. And later on he told me Borstal was the poor man's public school.

Brendan's imprisonment in England was shock enough for us all, but we had to live with it. He came back to us at Christmas 1942, having served about two years. Within a few months he had been arrested again, after firing at a detective who was following a march at Glasnevin. I suffered seas of sorrow from that fellow. The police Special Branch had threatened to shoot him like a mad dog. The first we knew of the whole business was when the Special Branch superintendent came to the house and said, 'Your Brendan's as good as dead, Mrs Behan. We'll shoot on sight.' There was to be no warning.

I cried my eyes out until Stephen came in for his tea. When I told him what was the matter he didn't say anything, but just went out and walked the town until he found one of his old IRA butties who was in a position to have the order lifted. Stephen saved Brendan's life that time. I nearly collapsed when the trial came up, and Brendan was sentenced by the military court to fourteen years, but I was so glad that he was alive.

Mind you, although Brendan got fourteen years he only served four. He was released on an amnesty. De Valera got them all to sign a document that they would have nothing more to do with the IRA. Brendan was one of the last to sign. He went back in 1947 to our house, his great big bald head on him. The neighbours got the shock of their lives, and some of the local hooligans got an even bigger one. They used to sit on our garden wall calling me and Da everything, and you daren't say a word to them. Well, our Brendan leaped out on top of them. I needn't tell you they nearly died. He was like that convict Magwitch in Dickens: Bald, enormous, and with a roar like a town bull. They ran for their lives!

Well, as you may well know, I had rocked Brendan in the

cradle to the air of 'The Red Flag'. Even from a very early age he was mixed up in politics. He joined Fianna Eireann, an IRA young people's organization something like the Boy Scouts, when he was only seven. Then he went on to become a courier for the 2nd Battalion of the IRA when he was only twelve.

Wait till I give you a laugh – you know he was thrown out of the IRA? Brendan was thrown out of the IRA on the charge of carrying unofficial guns, but really he was suspected of being a Communist. Brendan used to tell me everything. He told me that they had sentenced him to death in his absence for refusing to carry out their orders and turn in his gun.

He laughed and said, 'I can only hope they carry out the sentence in my absence as well.' He put that in a play.

He got back into the IRA later – his own officers didn't want him, but the Belfast IRA did. He told me, 'I don't like the company of Belfast people. They are dour in the Irish sense, they are narrow-minded like the ghetto they live in on the Falls Road, but they are serious about this question of the English in Ireland, and I knew a lot of them. I went speaking to them and they said they would take me back in my own company if only I would stay quiet.'

Brendan also told me that they were so serious about the removal of the British that he could see the day when the war in the North would burn the whole house down – North and South – if there was no settlement. He wasn't far wrong, looking at the state that we are in today, was he?

All our relations were Republican – to understand Brendan you have to understand that. My first husband's mother was an even greater Republican than myself. I saw her in 1939, just before she went to England – she was about eighty then. I had had measles as a child, which had permanently damaged my sight, and she thought I was great – an old blind woman, as she called me, to get two husbands, where good-looking women could only get one if they were lucky.

Her house was full of papers – she had one of Lenin and the Russian Revolution, and then alongside that a copy of the

Catholic Herald. She told me she was going to England in a few months.

'You giving up this grand house?' said I. (She lived out along the Clontarf Road, you know.)

'I am,' says she.

'Well, that's a queer thing,' says I. 'You wanting to go to England after all you've said about them over the years. You to go and live amongst them at the end of your life!'

'I am going,' she says, 'to strike a blow for Ireland, and even if I am at the end of my life I am going to strike it.'

I burst out laughing, God forgive me. The sight of this poor old woman going off to fight the Empire would make a cat laugh.

Well, off she went, and her two daughters, Evelyn and Emily, with her, just before Christmas – we had a party the night before she left. She was as good as her word – it was a bomb from her house that started the bombing campaign in England in 1939. Some people over here were delighted: one man said in the Dail that every bomb that exploded over there raised his heart. Wasn't that a terrible thing to say? I said to that man when I met him at a party, 'You should remember that every British soldier is some poor mother's son.'

Still, Shaw said that a baby carriage couldn't afford to be too gentlemanly if it had to fight a fifteen-ton lorry. Old Mrs Furlong used to bless every bomb. Peggy legs, the old woman used to call the sticks of explosive – you know, after the sticks of sweets that we used to eat when we were children. Queer old peggy legs. One of her daughters let a stick of gelignite fall out of a box and it blew up.

They were all arrested, along with a man – it was all in the papers. He was condemned to twenty years, Emily to five years, Evelyn to two years and Mary Ann Furlong herself to three years. She was muttering to herself when the judge called her to stand up so that he could read her penalty.

'Stand up for His Lordship,' said the court clerk.

'Wait a minute,' said she. 'I'm saying the Angelus, if you ever heard of it.'

'Now,' said she when she was ready. 'What do you want to say to me?'

He said that he had to condemn her to three years of penal servitude, and that she was as bad as the men.

'That's what I always heard,' said she, turning away without looking at him at all.

'Up the Republic,' said Martin, wrestling with the keepers.

'Encore, encore, after that,' said the old woman, walking proudly down the stairs to begin her three years.

It was after that that Brendan went off to England himself and followed in her footsteps. Do you know he said a funny thing to me one time? All his life he had been taught to hate the English, yet later on he wouldn't hear a bad word spoken against them. He claimed they were the finest people he ever had the pleasure to live among.

When he came out of Dublin jail after his sentence for shooting at the policeman he went over to England one last time. He helped some others to get Dick Timmons out of jail. Timmons was in for fourteen years, you know, for explosives. Brendan was caught, but they only charged him with breaking his deportation order, not the other thing. He did a couple of weeks and then came home. People tell how they had a great big dance the night our Brendan came home. He was the hero of the hour, and when he came into the dance hall you could hear a pin drop. Then they broke out in cheering that you could hear in Belfast.

Our Brendan spent so long in jail, he wrote a lot about it. He wrote a lovely song to go with his play *The Quare Fellow*, and called it 'The Old Triangle', after the metal triangle that used to be rung to call the prisoners to their tasks. Well, it was beginning to ring for our golden boy, and he was to hear its mournful music for many a day.

> A hungry feeling came o'er me stealing
> And the mice were squealing in my prison cell,
> And that old triangle
> Went jingle jangle,
> Along the banks of the Royal Canal.

To being the morning
The warder bawling
Get out of bed and clean up your cell,
And that old triangle,
Went jingle jangle,
Along the banks of the Royal Canal.

There's another verse, about women:

> In the female prison there are seventy women
> And amongst them I do long to dwell.
> Then that old triangle
> Would go jingle jangle
> Along the banks of the Royal Canal.

When Brendan was shifted from prison in Dublin to an internment camp in 1944 I felt much relieved. It was far better than prison. It was outside the city, down on the plains of Kildare, near the Curragh – it's a great racecourse as well. The internment camp was just a lot of huts surrounded by barbed wire. Brendan was happy enough – in the same way as Borstal, he called it 'the finishing school' or 'the poor man's university'.

One thing about Brendan – he hated to waste his time. He would always quote Shakespeare to me: 'Once I wasted time, now time wastes me.' He made the best of his opportunities inside or outside jail. He was much freer in the camp. There were no cells, just coming and going as you pleased between the huts. They had plenty of sport and could learn languages. Brendan became a very good Gaelic-speaker in there.

They filled the camps up with all sorts: some IRA and some like Neal Gould. His people had been very grand, the Goulds of Donegal, great landed people. But he wanted to give up all his money and live amongst the people as a humble man, just like our blessed Saviour Jesus Christ. Gould was so good. He lived in Crumlin with us for a time. Poor man – he had founded a tenants' committee there in the thirties and the common people worshipped the ground he walked on. The parish priest denounced him off the altar, and read out his name three times as the Antichrist, but the people didn't care.

In the early forties he tried to start a peasants' republic. He set up some tar barrels in the middle of the street in Dundalk and called on the people to rally round. They thought he was mad, and Gould was arrested. He was a very well-educated man. The judge at his trial said it was a shame and a disgrace that a man educated at Oxford and Cambridge, speaking ten languages, should appear before him on such a charge. Gould had been in Russia, but Stalin deported him.

In the camp he started to teach the lads Russian and Marxism. The bigwigs of the IRA said he was a Russian spy, but Brendan and the rest, those that supported the Anti-Hitlerites, refused to allow the IRA to throw him back over the wire. Some of the IRA wanted Hitler to win, but more of them, like Brendan, wanted to see him in Hell first. So they supported Gould and his teachings.

When he came out Gould gave all his money to the left-wing movement and then they expelled him. He went back to Russia after that, and we heard no more about him.

Brendan ate like a turkeycock in the camp. They had the same rations as the soldiers who were guarding them – Rory amongst them. Wasn't it funny, his own half-brother guarding the camp that held Brendan? Some of the IRA thought they were too comfortable, and should be suffering for the cause. They told Brendan they wanted to burn down the huts as a protest. He thought they were crackers! Well, burn them down they did, and if they made their beds they had to lie on them, in the snow. The Army commandant said they could lie there forever for all he cared.

My family was divided by the war. Seamus had joined the RAF, Brian and Rory (as you'll just have gathered) the Free State Army. The only ones at home now were Carmel and Dominic and Sean, who had been deported back from England. With Da more or less in constant work we were much better off. The only thing was the rations. We used to sing again:

The Family Breaks Up

God bless De Valera and Sean MacEntee
For giving us brown bread and a half-ounce of tea.

Coal you couldn't get for love nor money, only brown turf.

All my sons came back home by the end of the 1940s and for a time we had a happy, united family again. They were all working and we had plenty of money. I used to marvel on a Saturday as they handed up their wages. I was quids in.

Sean and Brian started a socialist co-op. They decided to sell turf. Well, they had to buy a great big horse and a cart. The trouble was they bought the cart before the horse, and when they brought the horse to the cart it wouldn't fit between the shafts. They had to make another set, but these were so heavy that the weight of them nearly brought poor Polly to her knees. Then the horse they bought was an anarchist – half mad and determined to do nothing. She ran away with Sean once, nearly killing him. The lads knew nothing of horses, you know.

One night Da came home to find this heap of turf piled up to the windows – the lads couldn't sell it in the middle of summer. The whole thing collapsed. But they were at least trying their best to get their living in Ireland. Above all else, they didn't want to emigrate. I was determined that they could go where they liked, but work they must. I told Brian to get a job and he said, 'There's no work in Dublin, Mother.'

I pointed to an advertisement in the *Evening Mail*. 'There's plenty of work in England,' says I, 'for them that wants it.' But they were good lads, all of them.

Brian started a union for farm workers and they had a very big strike. He was arrested for conspiracy and had to stand trial at Green Street Central Court. Then Dominic led a huge movement of the unemployed: people sitting down, choking all the city traffic. Baton charges were made on the unemployed, until finally they won the hearts of the people. They ended up electing the first unemployed Member of Parliament – a carpenter, Jack Murphy.

So our house was a constant stream of IRA, anarchists, socialists and all. We used to have meetings going on day and night. The locals called it the Kremlin. Da called it a madhouse and wished they could do their saving somewhere else.

Rory, my eldest son, was the first to leave. He got married, and I let him have our little front room in Crumlin, but in the end they had to go. Then Brendan left and went to live in the Catacombs, a dirty place full of drunkards like himself and low women. He used to stay there because he said it was too far to come home to Crumlin. Whatever the reason, Da told him to make up his mind, come or go, but do one thing or the other. All the trouble you have with children – rearing them, feeding them – and when they're old enough they're as bold as brass.

One Sunday Brendan took me and Da down there with him and I sang a lot of the old 'come all ye's'.

I'm a thumping fine widow, I live in a spot,
In Dublin they call it the Coombe.
Me shop and me stall are both out in the street
And me palace consists of one room.
At Patrick Street corner for twenty-five years
I've stood there, I'm telling no lie,
And while I stood there, nobody could dare
Say black was the white of me eye.
Ye may travel from Clare to the County Kildare
From Galway right back to Mac Croom.
But where will you see a fine widow like me.
Biddy Mulligan, the pride of the Coombe me boys
Biddy Mulligan, the pride of the Coombe.

I sell apples and oranges, nuts and split peas,
Bananas and sugar stick sweet,
I sell second-hand goods of a Saturday night,
And me stall is the floor of the street.
I sell fish on a Friday laid out on a dish,
Cod fish, aye, and wonderful ray,
I sell mackerel and herrings, lovely fresh herring
What once lived in dear Dublin Bay.

I have a son Michael who plays on the fife.
He belongs to the Longford Street Band.
'Twould do your heart good on a Saturday night
To see him march after the band.
In the park of a Sunday I quite cut a dash.
All the neighbours look on in surprise.
At me grand Paisley shawl, and me bonnet so tall
'Twould dazzle the sight of your eyes.
Ye may travel from Clare to the County Kildare
From Galway right back to Mac Croom,
But where will you see a fine widow like me –
Biddy Mulligan, the pride of the Coombe.

Brendan was great sport to be with. He could take off anyone, Pope or peasant, lord or down-and-out. At one party he was pretending to be an Irish pilgrim in Rome with two false hands outstretched in front of him, while with the other two he picked pockets. Da and I laughed until we cried. At the end of it Brendan raised a glass of stout and shouted out, 'Eff the begrudgers!' He begrudged nothing to life, did our Brendan.

7

The Famous and Infamous Behans

'You might as well sing grief as cry it.'

During the fifties and sixties the world was to hear much of the Behans. Brendan, flamboyant as ever, was most in the public eye with the success of *Borstal Boy* and plays such as *The Quare Fellow* and *The Hostage*, but Brian and Dominic, both writers, and Kathleen herself, now well known as a folk singer, also made their mark. Alcoholism was now taking its toll on Brendan, and he died in 1964, followed by Stephen in 1967

It was in the fifties that Brendan started to get well known. I think television helped make him: he was a child of the box. I often wondered what would have happened to our Brendan if there had been no television. In a way it killed him, too. You know, when he was drunk on the *Malcolm Muggeridge Show*, people thought he was great. One man said to me afterwards, 'I saw the Brendan Behan Show last night on television.' God help his sense, he thought it was our Brendan's show – not a word about Malcolm Muggeridge! But a lot of Brendan's drinking was put on, you know, a lot of codology to fool the natives. He told me about the show. He'd been determined that after it no one would ever forget the name Behan, and he made sure they didn't.

If he had never written a word, he could have earned his living as an actor. His uncle, Paddy Bourke, kept him supplied with regular free tickets to the Theatre Royal, and Brendan would spend hours imitating the people on the stage. His foreman brought him home to me from work one day when he was an apprentice, because he kept the rest of the men from working, entertaining them with his acts. The foreman said he would have to choose one thing or the other, play-acting or painting. I heard Malcolm Muggeridge say on television that he made the legend of Brendan Behan. Nothing could be further from the truth. Brendan was determined to hold sway in the world, and Muggeridge was only a stepping stone.

Although we were to become a very famous family, we were

also, as I have said, breaking up. What with one thing and
another, the fifties saw our little house empty. I had told the
lads often enough, 'It's not *your* home.' I had thought we – me
and Da, that is – would be on the pig's back when they went.
Well, we were in a way, but then again it was very lonely.

Probably no one would have heard anything about us but for
Brendan. He swung the world by the tail, I tell you. He took us
all over to England to look at the first night of *The Hostage*. We
stayed with the Guinness family, Lady Oranmore and Brown
and their son Tara – he was killed in a car crash, a fine lovely
lad. We went to *The Hostage* in style: we arrived in a Rolls and
came back in a Daimler.

You would think Brendan would be happy, but he wasn't.
You know he had always suffered from his nerves. He got that
from me – I used to die every week, as Rory would say when
they were all young. They sent for the priest so often he got
tired giving me the last rites. He asked Brendan to pray beside
my bed in Kildare Road, and Brendan just started reciting the
dirty bits out of *The Midnight Court** at him. Some of it's in
Gaelic, but you know, the poem's a terrible attack on the
Church altogether. Sure, the priest thought he was in the
hands of madmen, and ran for his life. He was surrounded by
the boys, with Brendan yelling out the *Courte bhan oidce* as
loud as he could!

Well, on the night of *The Hostage* he was all nerves again. He
just sat in the back of the Rolls and looked awful. He could
turn on you very quick, you know. That must have come from
Da – I never bore ill will in my life. Well, there in the Rolls he
turned on poor Brian and tore the flesh off his bones.

'You dirty renegade,' says he, 'to leave the Communist
Party when men like the poet MacDiarmid are going back into
it!'

Brian told him he should join as well, instead of being a rich
Red.

---

*A long satirical poem in Gaelic, written by Brian Merriman in 1796. Brendan is
reputed to have translated it, but to have mislaid the manuscript after a pub brawl
(*Ed.*)

Well, the language of our Brendan! How did the Guinnesses put up with it? Anyway, then he started abusing them too, saying Guinness was good for them but not for anyone else.

Well, when we finally got to the theatre I persuaded Brian to stay in the car, and in we went.

Up comes a man to Brendan: 'How are you, Brendan?' he says.

'Eff off,' says Brendan.

Wasn't that terrible? I never reared any son of mine to talk like that, and I told him so.

Well, he turned on *me* then.

I just listened, and then I said quietly, 'I will be off, then. I would never let *my* bone go to the dog.' If he didn't want his own mother there, good enough.

But then he quietened down, and we had a lovely evening after that.

You know, the press praised *The Hostage* to the skies. One man said we should treasure Brendan and be proud of him. I think it was Harold Hobson in the *Sunday Times*. Princess Margaret went down to Stratford to look at it and nearly died laughing. After that Brendan could do no wrong. I showed him all the papers and he just laughed. 'Mother,' says he, 'they would praise my balls if I hung them high enough.' Wasn't that terrible language to use to his own mother?

But Brendan really cared about the theatre. He said a city without a theatre was like a man without eyes. Mind you, he could be savage about plays he didn't like. He once described a climax to one scene as being about as dramatic as the clashing together of two dishclothes.

There again, when Brian was on strike in his famous South Bank dispute in London* it was Brendan hoiked me and Gerry Raffles of the Theatre Royal, Stratford East, and two other West End beauties into a great open car, and away down to the strikers. The strike was the talk of London. The papers called it the Battle of Waterloo because it was on the South Bank near

*Brian, working as a bricklayer and at this time a Communist, was the leader of a successful strike at the Shell Centre on London's South Bank development (*Ed.*)

Waterloo Station. Brian had just refused to allow the King and Queen on that same site to appear before the works committee. The papers had a cartoon showing him sitting on top of the dome with a bomb in his hand and, under it, 'Red Dawn on the Dome of Discovery'. Brendan was delighted.

We flew down in this car, and Brendan went round inspecting the pickets. I heard him say to Brian, 'I am proud of what you're doing.' The crowds of the world were there – thousands and thousands – and it was black with police. After that our Brendan went into a pub, dipped a flute into a glass of beer and played it to the crowds waiting outside a theatre. The money he collected – and it was a lot – he gave straight to the strikers. You wouldn't know what to make of him – one minute a saint, the next a devil.

After that I went on television for the BBC's *Tonight* programme. It was my first time on telly – we didn't even have one at home in Dublin then. Da was annoyed, because they didn't ask *him*. Well, the interviewer thought he had me. Before the show he got me to say what awful trouble I had had with my sons, particularly Brian. But when I went on, you should have seen his face!

'Mrs Behan,' says he, 'you must have suffered seas of sorrow in rearing this crew. Didn't you have a lot of trouble, especially with your son Brian?'

'Not a bit of it,' said I, 'You couldn't wish for a better set of sons. They couldn't be better to me. They never forget to send me money any week in their life.'

Well, he nearly died. He coughed, spluttered, and then he said, 'But what about all these strikes your son Brian is organizing over here?'

'Well,' says I, 'what about them? Sure the working man never got anything without fighting for it, did he?'

All during the fifties Dominic and Brendan were at each other's throats. I couldn't bear it. No mother wants to see her sons against each other. I told them, 'Don't fight. Don't beat each other. The world will beat you both long enough.' The family that's united can do anything, can't it?

I told them when they were little about the man with the bundle of sticks on his deathbed. He called his quarrelling sons before him and said, 'Now break those sticks.'

He had two bundles, one loose – well, they broke the loose sticks easily enough. But when they came to the tied bundle they tried, and couldn't.

'There,' he cried at them. 'Let you be the same. Stand together and no one will ever get the better of you.'

Our Dominic and Brendan were in the same two trades – painters and then writers. Whenever their paths crossed the insults would fly. And so it went on. The press loved it, of course. Dominic had a play on at the Metropole, *The Patriot Game*. We were all there, but Brendan walked out in the middle, shouting that it was an insult to the dead generations of Republicans that had fought and fallen for their country.

We all had dinner before the rehearsal of the play, but Brendan drank far too much. He just fell asleep, and then woke up roaring, 'It's a load of nonsense. There were no murderers in the IRA!'

Our Dominic shouted out, 'You were the worst murderer of the lot!'

There was a terrible row, with me and Da trying to make peace between them. It was the drink. He was drinking so much. He used to drink with that other fellow like Brendan – Dylan Thomas. He said he wasn't a poet at all, just a Welsh alley cat screeching. But *he* said more than his prayers, as you well know.

After that Brendan became very ill: this was in 1960. He went into the Middlesex Hospital in London. David Astor, who was Editor of the *Observer*, later wrote a lovely piece about our Brendan. Here it is:

I was a great admirer of Brendan from the time I read *Borstal Boy* and saw his plays. *The Quare Fellow* and *The Hostage* didn't have West End productions, but they tremendously impressed me. He will always be for me one of the great talents of his time.

I determined to meet him and, as a newspaper man, found a way of getting to know him. I found him in no way disappointing and we became friends. Incidentally, his drinking then was less catastrophic than it later became.

When, later, I began to realize that he would soon kill himself by drinking if he did not make a dramatic change, I felt I had to try to convey this to him. I visited him once in the Middlesex Hospital, where he was in the psychiatric ward. This was an open ward, but I nevertheless asked him to say yes or no whether he wanted to take a cure for alcoholism – I said I knew there was at least one hospital in London that specialized in this problem. Brendan gave an ambiguous answer. Yes, he would like to be cured, but, no, he would not face life in a hospital for alcoholics. Why? He said words to the effect that it would be an invasion of his privacy. We left it there.

When he came out, I invited him to have a serious talk about his fate. I even asked him to visit my office to emphasize that it was not a social occasion. He came with Beatrice, whom I met for the first time and greatly liked, although it was hard not to feel a sense of tragic foreboding about her.

At that time, *The Observer*'s medical correspondent was Dr Abraham Marcus, whose family came from Cork and whose brother edited a literary magazine in Dublin. He naturally knew Brendan's personal story, and Brendan knew of him. I asked him to be with me when Brendan visited. Bram Marcus was always very direct, speaking out clearly and without too much diplomacy. He opened up the conversation by asking Brendan in the simplest but most humane terms if he understood that he would surely die in the fairly near future if he did not give up the drink completely. Brendan did not answer equally simply. But he did not dispute what Marcus said. It was also made clear to Brendan that he could not expect to give up alcohol if he did not put himself in the hands of a doctor and agree to live in a hospital for a certain time.

It is nonsense to think, as some jealous people have done, that his drinking was an attempt to blow up a minor talent or deliberately play at being a genius. His talent was, I believe, far greater than the media ever appreciated. But it did not include a gift for peace of mind or contentment. It seemed as though he wanted to kill an inner demon, some troubled state he could not live down. I remember him once saying, quietly and a little sadly. 'I'm not the enjoying kind.' He didn't drink for pleasure, but as a means of execution. But the fact that the drink killed not only the inner demon but the whole man cannot detract from his great talents as an artist.

He was also a very honest and an unpretentious man. I heard him once remark to his audience on television, 'Why on earth are you looking at this load of rubbish – you'd be far better off taking a walk round the block.' I've never heard anyone else talk like this to the viewers.

His contempt for the media was genuine enough. He abused them and they exploited him. But they didn't kill him. He died because of his own inner demons, whatever they were.

I last met him in a private nursing home in the Cromwell Road. We spoke of our families. He had heard of my mother and was interested in her. I never saw him again.

Well, how could I get Brendan to do anything if he didn't want to do it? Shortly after that he gave up the drink anyway, because he wanted to, and because he was married to Beatrice.

At the end of 1960 he told me he was off to America with a woman. 'Jesus, Mary and Joseph,' I said to myself. 'He's left Beatrice!' But it wasn't that at all, I discovered later. He was off with Rae Jeffs of Hutchinson to write two books. Well, before he left he took me, Beatrice,* Rae Jeffs and Aunt Maggie on a lightning tour of Ireland. He gave us a big lunch at Glendalough. Da used to sing a song about the saint and his temptations there, called 'In Glendalough Lived an Old Saint'.

> In Glendalough lived an old saint
> Who passed all his days in austerity.
> His fashions were curiously quaint
> And he looked upon girls with severity.
> *Singing fol-de-lol-do-de-lay,*
> *Right-fol-do-de-dol-de-lid-dady,*
> *Singing fol-de-lol-do-de-lay,*
> *Right-fol-do-de-dol-de-lil-dady.*

*Brendan had married Beatrice ffrench-Salkeld in 1955 (*Ed.*)

He was fond of reading a book,
When he could get one to his wishes.
He was fond of swinging a hook
Down among the old fishes.
Refrain.

As he was fishing one day
Kathleen from over the way, sir.
She came right into his way
To see what the old saint was about, sir.
Refrain.

Get out of my way, says the saint,
For I am a man of great piety.
My good manners I wouldn't taint
Mixing in female society.
Refrain.

But Kathleen wasn't going to give in,
And when he went home to his tea, sir,
Oh, there she was seated within,
Ready to meet him again, sir.
Refrain.

Well, he gave the poor creature a shove,
I wished that a bobby had caught him.
He threw her right into the lake,
And she fell right down to the bottom.
Refrain.

Anyway, when we got there we had a lovely hour. The hotel overlooks the lakes and you couldn't wish for a better place. The mountains were all around us, and the air like wine.

Brendan insisted that we get up and go to another set of lakes nearly two hundred miles away in Kerry. I said, 'You're mad!' and we all sat down again. Well, we were drinking fairly freely and one word borrowed another. I didn't know at this time who or what Rae Jeffs was – I thought they were going off to America together. Only afterwards did I know that Beatrice was going as well. Well, I shouted over to Rae, who was

English, 'You killed Kevin Barry.'

I don't think she heard me, but Brendan just shouted at me, 'Leave that girl alone! She knows nothing about these things.'

And then to make it all up I sang 'Kevin Barry'. You know the song: 'Just a lad of eighteen summers who walked to death that morning.' Well, Rae, was crying by the time I had finished, and all was well. Brendan put his arm around me and apologized for eating my head off a bit earlier.

Then we went back to Crumlin and Da wouldn't let Brendan in. He was jealous, I suppose, that we hadn't asked him. Well, Brendan just pushed by him and I vanished up to bed. I have always found bed best when storm clouds gather. I could hear Da arguing and Brendan shouting that his family should respect his talent.

Da said, 'You should have more respect for them that kept you.'

Brendan said very cuttingly – he had a tongue like a hatchet, 'You *had* to keep us. It's against the law to starve children!'

What a terrible way to end a lovely day.

People thought Brendan had been a pet son of *mine*, but that wasn't so. Brendan always used my songs and stories in his plays, but he never really gave Da the credit that he should have. Da was forever reading to us all, and always took Brendan's part outside the house. Brendan didn't know it, but often Da was in a fight with people who belittled Brendan. I liked meeting the Guinnesses and the Astors, but Da never really felt at ease with them.

Later, after Brendan returned from the USA, was the worst day of my life up to that time. He walked out of the house, and he was found in the early hours of the morning lying in a pool of his own blood. He was rushed to hospital. Some of the dirty gurriers of Dublin had beaten him unconscious. Da was heartbroken. It wasn't his fault, but Brendan never set foot in our house again after that – in any house, for that matter, even his wife's. Da was content to drink beer. Brendan was for the champagne of life. There's the difference for you.

Brendan used to say, 'I want to die when I am ninety with a

mountain of pillows behind me, and sixty priests and forty nuns praying fervently I will go to Heaven.' He told me he was a daytime atheist and a night-time Catholic. Beatrice told me his life could have been saved. There was a good chance that if he had an operation to the brain he could have lived to fifty at least. But he thought if he had the operation he might go mad. He had a fear of madness, you know. Good reason, too. He had a terrible temper. You couldn't get him to do anything he didn't want to do. So he never had the operation which might have saved him. Though maybe it was all for the best. He could never bear to think of himself as an invalid, which he was, near the end.

There's a song about death, you know. It's in his play *The Hostage*.

> The bells of hell
> Go ting-a-ling-a-ling
> For you but not for me.
> Oh death where is thy
> Sting-a-ling-a-ling
> Or grave thy victory?
> If you meet the undertaker
> Or the young man from the Pru,
> Get a pint with what's left over.
> Now I'll say goodbye to you.

Brendan died on 19 March 1964. March 1984 will be the twentieth anniversary of his death, if it pleases God to let me see it.

I remember the day quite well. Da and I went to the Meath Hospital with John Ryan. (John wasn't to be allowed in – only close relatives. Then he pretended to be Rory and got in. Rory couldn't get in later on over the mix-up, though I think he did, eventually.)

When I looked at Brendan, I thought my heart would break, if it wasn't broken already. His lovely brown hair tumbling down. I knew his race was run. I said to John, 'He won't live beyond this afternoon.' We went back to the Bailey and had a

126

drink – you may as well sing grief as cry it – and Brendan wouldn't have wanted us to sit there moping. Well, they rang us at the Bailey and told us our Bengy was dead. Our golden boy. My little poet. My heart, my life. I had seven sons, then one died, but I still thought I had six to carry my coffin. Now there were five. There is no love like a mother's. There is not a single day I haven't thought about him and all my little ones. Well, He knows the clay of which we are formed. I am sure Brendan is with our Blessed and Holy Mother in Heaven. When he was little I thought, how like a little angel he is. Now he is gone forever.

Come here till I tell you a story about Brendan when he was a little lad. I just want you to see how little he changed.

He was five years old when this happened, and we were living in a tenement. He toddled out of the house and rambled in next door, where a neighbour was giving breakfast to her family. She had just put on some eggs to cook when she saw this extra little visitor coming in. She sat him down, but she couldn't afford to cook an egg for little Brendan so she poured him a cup of tea and buttered some bread for him.

Brendan sat for a while staring disconsolately at his plate, not touching a thing. When the neighbour said to him, 'Have you lost your appetite, child – will you not eat up your breakfast?' our little Brendan looked at the lad beside him and said, 'Hello, egg.'

Even at that age, he had more sense of humour than most men develop in a lifetime.

Brendan was such a great man. His sense of humour was with him from the day he was born, and never left him to the day he died. He was full of fun and songs. It's nice to see Brendan remembered. He was a man that loved everyone. He was always good to the old folk and he loved little children. When he used to throw pennies for children, and later on it was shillings and half crowns, he used to get anxious in case some of the little ones wouldn't manage to get any of the money.

I always liked *Borstal Boy*, because it's Brendan as he was to me – forgiving and good-natured. *The Hostage* was great too, but *The Quare Fellow* was a little bit sad, I think. My favourite part in *Borstal Boy* is where he's serving at Mass. Brendan used to be an altar boy, you know.

I want to pay tribute to my son. Brendan always stood by his friends. He let no one down in a real sense. He lived a gay, wild, extravagant, loud life. He never counted the cost. He died a far too early death. But who will cast the first stone? Is it better to die young having led a full life and leaving behind *Borstal Boy* and *The Quare Fellow* than to die quietly at four score leaving behind a handful of dust?

In the sixties we went to England quite a lot. We would have moved there, but Da might not have got a job. He was getting on in years then, and in 1967 he died.

In 1966 Brian won a mature student scholarship to Sussex University and was as pleased as punch. One of his professors said, 'I don't know what the university can do for you, Mr Behan, but I am sure you can offer a very great deal.' I went over to England to celebrate and nearly got shot.

I was staying on Brian's houseboat at the time, and went to the loo. It was a funny old ship's loo and Brian had newly painted the seat. Well, you know what happened? I was stuck there good and proper. It was lucky I was, for at that moment about six shots rang out and hit the boat. I nearly died of fright. Brian had an American sculptress staying with him – she was nearly wounded in the leg. It was in all the papers next day. She's the woman who made the concrete cows of Milton Keynes. Well, the papers had banner headlines: 'Sussex Detectives Hunt for Behan Assassin.'

I asked an old police superintendent what chance they had.

'None,' said he, smiling. 'My dear woman, the gunman could have been half a mile away. It was from a high-powered rifle.'

It might have been some husband after Brian, for he lived a wild life on the boats. One of them was so bad, the local council tried to burn it as an example to the rest. Making love on the deck, brazen lot! I asked Brian why he had so many young women on board.

'It's a home for distressed women,' says he.

'Well, if they are not distressed when they arrive, they will be before they leave you,' I replied.

He was like his father. You couldn't trust Da even now with a young woman, and he's been dead nearly twenty years.

As I said, Brian was off to university. I begged him to attend to his studies and not miss a great opportunity. Isn't England a great country, that it could give a poor labouring boy like Brian the chance to go at all? In Ireland that would not happen. The sky would turn blue, pigs would fly, before they would allow the sons or daughters of the poor to join them at Trinity. My lads would never have seen the sky over a university in Ireland, even though they were as clever as the cleverest professors – though I hear that Con Kearney's son is a professor now. Colbert, his name is – he's at Cork University. So maybe things *are* changing after all. I am talking about years ago, and being in here, in this home, time and events pass you by.

Well, Brian didn't like me talking like that to him.

'Straighten your back,' I said, 'when you get in there. Otherwise they will think you're an old man.'

If looks could have killed I would have been a dead woman. 'Mother,' says he, 'I am not going to waste my time. I do not believe in wasting other people's money.'

'Brian,' says I, 'it's your own mother you're talking to now.'

'Even so,' says he, 'I am not going to count the hairs on Trotsky's beard.'

'Sure,' I said, 'I don't know who Trotsky is. He sounds like a horse.'

Epilogue

Kathleen . . . and when will you come again, Brian?

Brian I will come and see you in the autumn, Mother.

Kathleen If God spares me. Remember what I said. You will all have to make a collection to bury me. I am insured for very little.

Brian But I thought you had £2000 over and above your pension for the accident money?

Kathleen Sure, I spent that.

Brian (outraged) On what?

Kathleen On drink and dancing and singing so merrily!

Brian It seems a lot to spend on top of your old age pension, and you getting your food in here.

Kathleen Sure, £2000 wouldn't go anywhere these days.

Brian Are you afraid of death?

Kathleen No, I wouldn't be afraid to die.

Brian You used to say that working-class women would go to Heaven before nuns.

Kathleen And they will. Nuns lock themselves away from the cares of the world. They have neither chick nor child.

Brian On a Sunday Da used to shout out to us in bed, 'Go out and meet your God, you lazy pack of hounds!' Are you sure there's a God to meet?

Kathleen Even if we come back as seeds, isn't that better than nothing?

I'll be singing a song when I'm dying, an old 'come all ye'. Last night we were in a pub down here locally, and they were all talking about dogs and cats. They only allow us to sing on Friday, Saturday and Sunday, but when they were talking about the dogs, didn't I sing 'My Daddy Wouldn't Buy Me a Bow-wow'? We had the best of laughs.

I don't want any tears when I'm gone. Enjoy yourselves, I say to my friends and relatives. Give me a decent funeral. Any money that's left over – have a good drink. You must all be happy, say she's gone to Heaven. I hope. You should sing and dance. I've had a very happy life, thank God – lovely husbands and lovely children. I've had three lovely birthdays – 90, 91 and 92. Here's a song you can all sing when I'm gone.

> Hey ho *slainte* the revelry,
> The singing and dancing and drinking so merrily,
> Red nights, which we never again will see,
> For down in the village we tarried too long . . .

An Appreciation of Kathleen
by Beatrice Behan

I first met Kathleen on the day of my wedding in Kennedy's off Harold's Cross, a pub just by the canal. There were five of us that morning: my father, Cecil, who was driving us, Celia, my sister, Reg Grey, the best man, and Brendan and myself.

We had called at the house on Kildare Road to collect Kathleen, but she had gone shopping. We met her later on the road with her shopping bag and messages. Brendan asked my father to stop the car and called to her: 'Come on, Mother, we're going for a few drinks.' We went to Kennedy's bar and it wasn't long before Kathleen was singing. She had a beautiful voice and a repertoire of songs the like of which I had never heard before.

In those days she was a tall, spare woman with large, expressive hands that moved in time with her songs. Never before had I met someone who could sing so many ballads, and now I knew where Brendan got his great singing voice, a voice that in those days could silence the noisy chatter of an entire bar. At one stage Kathleen chided, 'Brendan, you shouldn't be cursing in front of those lovely young girls.' She laced her conversation with Irish expressions like '*Alann mo chroi* (child of my heart)', or '*Slainte agus fad saol* (health and long life to you)', the Irish toast which Brendan also used – only his was a much longer and ribald version.

She got on very well with my father, for they had known many people in common: Maud Gonne MacBride, for whom Kathleen worked for a while, and William Butler Yeats, who

133

was a frequent visitor to the house in St Stephen's Green. It came to 2.30 (the Holy Hour), and we were asked to leave. Reluctantly we left the bar and I bade farewell to Kathleen of the songs. What I never knew about that day was that she had no idea that we had just been married. We often laughed about it, years later. My father went home by taxi with Celia and Reg, so the following day he was convinced he'd lost his car. Brendan and I set sail for France that night. It had been a day to remember.

Our first flat after we were married was in Waterloo Road in Dublin. Once a week Brendan would go to the fish market. Sometimes when he came home he'd say, 'Bring some of that fish up to my mother.' So I would cycle up the canal to 70 Kildare Road with the fish for Kathleen – whiting, ray or herrings. We would have tea together and lovely brown bread or scones which she had baked herself. She was a great hand at baking and I would come home with a brown cake or a batch of scones. I never left her house without something, whether it was something she had baked, or a pair of hand-knitted socks for Brendan, or perhaps a little piece of china for the flat. While we had our tea Kathleen would talk about herself, her family, and how she met and married Stephen, whom she used to meet at musical evenings with her first husband, Jack Furlong, who had died during the flu epidemic of 1918. Stephen was apparently a confirmed bachelor when Kathleen first knew him, but the young widow had set her heart on him. She told me with a twinkle in her eye, 'Sure, I thought I'd never get him.'

However, the courtship was not without its ups and downs. At that time Kathleen worked as a caretaker for the White Cross in Harcourt Street. On one of their first trysts near St Stephen's Green Kathleen cautiously peeped round a corner to see if her young man was there, waiting for her. He was, but to her absolute horror she noticed that he was wearing string as laces in his boots. 'Oh, the shame of it,' said Kathleen to herself, as she turned around and walked away. In spite of all, the courtship flowered and they were married in the University

Church, St Stephen's Green, in 1922. The young widow of twenty-eight with her two small children had married Stephen Behan. Their great adventure had begun.

After their marriage Stephen and Kathleen went to live at 14 Russell Street, the home of Stephen's mother, Mrs Christina English ('the Grannie'). Mrs English had been twice married, and by all accounts was quite a character herself. When a garrulous neighbour once remarked, 'Oh, Mrs English, I believe you were married twice?' her caustic reply was, 'Sure, any fool can get one man.' She lay in bed most days and from there reigned over her tenants like a queen, dispensing advice and porter in alternate doses.

Stephen Behan, known as Da to his wife and family, was a fine, dapper little man with neat, small hands. I first met him after my marriage to Brendan, one spring evening in Sinnott's pub. He was witty and charming and had a great laugh. Brendan had been the first child of the marriage. By all accounts he grew up to be a beautiful child with auburn curls and blue eyes, and was very spoiled by the Grannie as a result. As he so often told me, 'I was reared a pet.'

His childhood was a happy one, at school with the French Sisters of Charity in North William Street whom he loved. On warm summer days Kathleen would take her small children to the seaside at Dollymount. If she came across children playing with live crabs, she gave them sixpence for the crabs and then set them free. Sixpence was a lot of money in those times. She loved animals and had several dogs and cats in their house in Kildare Road, where she spent the later part of her life with her family of six sons and one daughter.

In the 1920s, Kathleen had a wide circle of friends. She had worked for Maud Gonne MacBride, knew Michael Collins well, and had met most of the Republican leaders. In the years when I first knew Kathleen one of her constant companions was a woman called Aunt Maggie who lived near her. I loved Aunt Maggie because she was dressed so prim and properly in Victorian style, and would come out with the most outrageous statements like: 'I'd love to get an old man with young ways', or 'Will you take it now, or wait till it's flying?' This was after she was widowed, I hasten to add.

Aunt Maggie had been married to Joe Trimble, a 1916 man whom I had met a few times. He was very tall and thin and he had been in the GPO in Easter Week. The story goes that Aunt Maggie went down O'Connell Street, with shot and shells flying in all directions. She crossed the barricades outside the GPO and shouted up at one of the shattered windows, 'Is Joe Trimble inside?

Someone shouted back at her, 'Ma'am, get back! Get back! You'll be riddled.'

Aunt Maggie ignored these warnings, and presently Joe appeared at the window, slightly embarrassed.

Maggie shouted up to him, 'All I want to know is, are you going to your work tomorrow, and if you are not, could you throw us out a few postal orders?'

Joe Trimble used to tell risqué stories. One day he said to Kathleen, 'Excuse me, Kathleen. I know you won't mind this story, as you're a married woman.'

Kathleen replied grandly, 'I may be a married woman, Joe, but I'm not a dustbin.'

When Kathleen was pregnant with Brendan, she met Michael Collins on O'Connell Street Bridge. He was a man with a price on his head, but stopped to talk with her. 'How are you, Kathleen, where are you living now? How are the children?' They chatted for a few minutes, and on leaving her he pressed a ten-pound note into her hand, saying, 'Take care of yourself.' It was the last time she ever saw him. To commemorate this incident, that happened before he was born, Brendan wrote a song in honour of Michael Collins called 'The Laughing Boy'. It is sung in *The Hostage* and is the first song that was ever written specially for Michael Collins.

'Twas on an August morning, all in the morning hours,
I went to take the warming air all in the month of flowers,
And there I saw a maiden and heard her mournful cry,
Oh what will mend my broken heart, I've lost my laughing boy.

So strong, so wide and brave he was, I'll mourn his loss too sore,
When thinking that we'll hear the laugh or springing step no more,
Ah, curse the time, and sad the loss my heart to crucify,
That an Irish son, with a rebel gun, shot down my laughing boy.

Oh, had he died by Pearse's side or in the GPO,
Killed by an English bullet from the rifle of the foe,
Or forcibly fed while Ashe lay dead in the dungeons of Mountjoy,
I'd have cried with pride at the way he died, my own dear laughing
   boy.

My princely love, can ageless love do more than tell to you
Go raibh mile maith Agath, for all you tried to do.
For all you did and would have done, my enemies to destroy,
I'll praise your name and guard your fame, my own dear laughing
   boy.

While Kathleen was working for Maud Gonne MacBride she
met Sarah Purser, who painted a beautiful portrait of her
which now hangs in the National Gallery of Ireland.*

   Today Kathleen is ninety-four, a fierce feminist and Republican (old IRA). As she says herself, she is never too sick or
too weary to sing a song for you. When I call to see her at St
Joseph's we talk about days gone by, people – alas – gone too,
and her family and friends. She will introduce you to her
friends in the home: Mary and Mrs Brown, and the young
Sister who looks after her. Sometimes the days must be long
for Kathleen, as they rise so early, though the last day I was
there she told me, 'I hate the bed. I have to get up. Isn't it a
pity there's no cure for old age?' Her sight has failed now, so
she cannot read any more, but she loves to listen to the radio.
'I'd be gone mad years ago without it,' she says. She only goes
to the television lounge to meet her friends and have a chat.

   Outside her window the whole circle of Dublin Bay stretches
glittering in the sunshine, while children laugh and play in the
gardens below. 'Draw the curtain, over, *alanna*, the sunlight
hurts my eyes,' she says. I ask her if she has any news. 'I'm

*See between pages 80 and 81.

alive, isn't that news enough for you?' she quips. Her spirit, her strength of will seem sustained by that great store of memories which must crowd back as she talks to me. And I see again the tall, auburn-haired woman walking arm in arm with her husband along St Stephen's Green, and I remember then how it was on Sunday nights when I first knew them: surrounded by all their admirers and friends – Rory and May Furlong, Pearse and Bridie Kearney, Aunt Maggie, Brendan and myself, and of course Paddy O'Brien, the genial barman and friend to all.

'Mother – sing "When All the World Was Young", Brendan would call out. It was one of his favourites.

So Kathleen would sing her version in her clear, strong voice:

> When all the world is young, lad,
> And all the trees are green,
> And every goose a swan, lad,
> And every lass a queen.
> You get upon your big white horse,
> And gaily ride away,
> For youth must have its fling, lad,
> And every dog his day.
>
> When all the world is old, lad,
> And all the trees are brown,
> And all your big high hopes come
> Trembling, tumbling down.
> Go you to your corner, lad,
> The spent and maimed among,
> God grant you will find one face there, lad,
> You loved when all the world was young.

AKÉ
Wole Soyinka

'What if V. S. Naipaul was a happy man? . . . What if Vladimir Nabokov had grown up in a small town in Western Nigeria and decided that politics were not unworthy of him? . . . *Aké* locates the lost child in all of us, underneath language, inside sound and smell, wide-eyed, brave and flummoxed. What Waugh made fun of and Proust felt bad about, Mr Soyinka celebrates . . . Brilliant'   John Leonard,
The Sunday Times

'A superb act of remembrance . . . dazzling reading . . . *Aké* has an enchanting effect . . . Soyinka's memoir makes everything seem wondrous'
Village Voice

'Enchanting' *The Observer*

ARENA

THE DREAD AFFAIR
Collected poems

Benjamin Zephaniah

FIGHT DEM
ESS DOUBLE YOU NINE (BRIXTON)
CAN'T KEEP A GOOD DREAD DOWN
NICE ONE HANDSWORTH
THE BOAT IS SINKING
GANJA ROCK
THE DAY DAT I MET LADY DI
DIS POLICEMAN KEEPS ON KICKING ME TO DEATH
etc.

THE DREAD AFFAIR

poems for now

Benjamin Zephaniah has a lot to say. His humour, anger, passion and contentiousness have already established him as one of the most important and popular of Britain's new wave of performing poets. His poems speak for themselves.

ARENA

ARENA

'Rumbustious . . . original . . . splendid'
The Guardian

CLANCY'S BULBA
Michael O'Gormon

On the floor huddled close together with blankets wrapped around them, lay Barra Duffy, Pagannini O'Leary and Milo Clancy, owners of the finest fighting cock in County Mayo. On the bed, sleeping in the centre of the mattress, was the champion himself, Taurus Bulba. Back home the men would have been in their beds and the cockerel in his shed. But all four souls were far from home now . . . Further away than any of them had ever been before, astounded by the unaccustomed splendour of Aggie Carney's White Willow Hotel, Duffy, O'Leary and Clancy come to realize that Taurus Bulba can do more for them than win the regional cock-fighting championship. He can take them out of the poverty and simplicity of their lives and into a land of dreams as well.

Too late will they realize just how much those dreams might cost . . .

Warm, sparkling and irrepressibly humorous, CLANCY'S BULBA is much more than 'a story about . . .'. Here myth and reality combine with extraordinary, free-wheeling dialogue to create a story that is as richly imagined and vividly drawn as it is original.

'Not often does a first book achieve such vigour of phrase or cut characters so sharp'   *Mail on Sunday*

ARENA

THY TEARS MIGHT CEASE
Michael Farrell

One of the great Irish novels of our time, *Thy Tears Might Cease* is the story of Martin Reilly, a young boy growing up in Ireland during the time of the troubles. Written with extraordinary insight and sensitivity, it is a brilliant evocation of the formative years of manhood, of the extremes of first love and of the pain of divided loyalties . . .

'A lyrical and beautiful book and a work of art in the fullest sense'   *Daily Telegraph*

'A work of real splendour' *Daily Mail*

ARENA

TWISTED KICKS
Tom Carson

In prose as precisely cut as the grooves of a stereo disc, and with the mesmeric intensity of rock itself, *Twisted Kicks* encapsulates the rock scene of the seventies – with its humour, its anguish, its brittle glory and its empty dreams. What F. Scott Fitzgerald did for the generation that claimed the twenties and Jack Kerouac did for the beat generation of the fifties, Tom Carson has now done for the seventies. Dan Lang is a rock musician who, fleeing from a killing in New York, returns to his home in Virginia to visit the old 'gang' and the past he cannot escape – and moves from one kind of jungle to another. *Twisted Kicks* is sex and drugs and rock 'n' roll – but more than that it is a powerful, almost hypnotic story of a society that no longer has anything to dream about.

'It doesn't seem enough to call this novel talented: it puts one in mind of early Hemingway or Nathaniel West'   *Publishers Weekly*

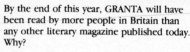